The Other Jesus

The Other Jesus

Rejecting a Religion of Fear
for the God of Love

GREG GARRETT

WESTMINSTER
JOHN KNOX PRESS
LOUISVILLE · KENTUCKY

First edition
Published by Westminster John Knox Press
Louisville, Kentucky

11 12 13 14 15 16 17 18 19 20—10 9 8 7 6 5 4 3 2 1

Except as otherwise identified, Scripture is from the *New Revised Standard Version Bible,* copyright 1989, by the Division of Christian Education of the National Council of the Churches of Christ in the USA, and is used by permission. The quote identified as NJB is from *The New Jerusalem Bible,* copyright © 1985 by Darton, Longman & Todd Ltd and Doubleday, a division of Bantam Doubleday Dell Publishing Group, Inc., and is reprinted by permission. KJV stands for the King James Version of the Holy Bible.

Compass of Affection
By Scott Cairns
© 2006 by Scott Cairns
Used by permission of Paraclete Press
www.paracletepress.com<http://www.paracletepress.com/>

Book design by Sharon Adams
Cover design by designpointinc.com
Cover art © The Holy Face by Juan Casco/Superstock

Library of Congress Cataloging-in-Publication Data

Garrett, Greg.
  The other Jesus : rejecting a religion of fear for the God of love / Greg Garrett.
      p. cm.
  ISBN 978-0-664-23404-1 (alk. paper)
  1. Theology, Doctrinal—Popular works.   I. Title.
  BT77.G36   2011
  230—dc22

                                                         2010034960

PRINTED IN THE UNITED STATES OF AMERICA

♾ The paper used in this publication meets the minimum requirements of the American National Standard for Information Sciences—Permanence of Paper for Printed Library Materials, ANSI Z39.48-1992.

Westminster John Knox Press advocates the responsible use of our natural resources. The text paper of this book is made from at least 30% postconsumer waste.

Special Sales
Most Westminster John Knox Press books are available at special quantity discounts when purchased in bulk by corporations, organizations, and special-interest groups. For more information, please e-mail SpecialSales@wjkbooks.com.

Contents

He is angry. He is just. And while
he may have died for us,
it was not gladly. The way
his prophets talk, you'd think
the whole affair had left him
queerly out of sorts, unspeakably
indignant, more than a little
needy, and quick to dish out
just deserts. I saw him when,
as a boy in church, I first
met souls in hell. I made
him for a corrupt, corrupting fiction when
my own father (mortal that he was)
forgave me everything, unasked.

Scott Cairns, from "The Spiteful Jesus"

Preface

As a writer, I rarely feel constrained to explain a book—if it doesn't do that all on its own, then I usually feel that I've failed, and I am always telling my students not to tell me what they've written, but just to let me read it.

But with a book like this, which at least appears to be making some dramatic claims, I feel that a few explanations are in order so readers can know exactly what I propose to do here.

First, I don't intend this book as a systematic theology, or at least not as a restrictive one. Although I will call attention to bad theology when I think I see it walking around in the world, my intention in writing *The Other Jesus* is not to establish what I believe are right and wrong parameters of belief; that seems to be a big part of what has gotten Christianity into the state it's in. Some people are perfectly happy with their faith and practice; some are incorporating parts of these emerging (and ancient) Christian understandings into their faith and practice; some want to burn the whole thing down and start over.

So though we are conditioned to avoid criticism of another's faith, it's only honest to say that what I am calling Christianity 1.0 (recognizing that it's a long way down the numerical scale—I just like the metaphor of upgrading to a better operating system) does not seem to be getting the job done for the twenty-first century. Sometimes, I fear, it doesn't even recognize what its job is. As my friend Scott Bader-Saye has written, "In the past when asked, 'What is your chief goal?' Christians have given answers such as 'friendship with God' ([Thomas] Aquinas, [thirteenth century]) or 'to glorify God and enjoy him forever' (Westminster Catechism, seventeenth century).

Today I suspect that many Christians would echo the culture in naming 'safety' or 'security' as the primary good they seek."[1] And safety and security may be valuable things, but in the Christian scheme of things, they're just not very important.

So we are going to explore problems, ask questions, and consider possibilities for what it might mean to be a thoughtful Christian in a complicated and sometimes frightening world. My hope is that you, the reader of this book, will wrestle with these questions and come to your own answers instead of just taking my word for things. Twenty-five years of being a college professor—and a parent—have taught me that "Because" is not a meaningful answer to the question "Why?" It's up to each of us to answer the challenging questions in ways that make personal sense; these are hard-won truths for me and for others, but you will have to own them for yourself.

So I'm not here as arbiter of truth; I am here as a tour guide with some distinctive bona fides. Through family, past history, or present circumstances, I have been involved in a number of different Christian traditions, including fundamentalist, evangelical, and mainline Christianity. I have personally attended (among others) Anglican, Assembly of God, Baptist, Bible Church, Catholic, Church of Christ, Emergent, Episcopalian, Lutheran, Methodist, Nazarene, Presbyterian, and Unitarian worship services. I have been a follower of a simplistic Christianity that ultimately repelled me; I have been a doubter, outside of any faith because of my perceptions of Christianity; I have become a believer in a Christian tradition that values all the things I value: intellect, beauty, ritual, spiritual practice, justice. Within that tradition, I have studied Christianity past, present, and future as a seminarian considering ministry in the church of the twenty-first century, and as a theologian trying to find a way forward for the faith that has changed my life.

In this book I want to present some possibilities for a dynamic, thoughtful Christianity that I have tested in the laboratory of life and found meaningful, or have seen expressed in the lives of others, possibilities that might be useful to a wide range of readers. If you are a seeker interested in what you know of Jesus but repelled by what you know of Christianity, this book is for you. If you are a member of a Christian tradition that, for whatever reason, has pushed you away from God instead of toward God, this book is for you. If you are an emergent

Christian looking for some ideas from the tradition about how to be faithful in a changing world, this book is for you. If you are a leader in a mainline tradition who needs to be reminded of what might bring vitality back into your faith and into your church, this book is for you. In each chapter I roll out some of the problems that contemporary Christianity seems to be facing, explore the Bible and the tradition to see what they have to say, refute what I think are bad teachings and foreground good ones, and suggest some practical ways forward. At the end of each chapter I've included discussion questions to spark your own inquiry and suggested some books that survey the chapter's issues in more detail. You can explore this book on your own, with a small group, or as a part of a larger group; I do hope that at some point these ideas don't simply bounce around in your head but get out and play with those of others.

In researching and writing this book, I have benefited from conversations and e-mail exchanges I have had in recent years with a number of Christian pastors and priests, leaders, writers, and thinkers. While they are certainly not to be blamed for anything with which you disagreed, they did (and do) help me to clarify my own ideas concerning Christian faith and practice in the twenty-first century. I am particularly grateful for interviews with two of the youngest (and most creative) bishops in the Episcopal Church, the Right Reverend Greg Rickel (Olympia), and the Right Reverend Andy Doyle (Texas), who allowed me to quiz them on matters that church leaders often would rather not discuss.

Others who have been a part of this conversation include Chris Seay, Brian McLaren, Phyllis Tickle, Philip and Ali Newell, Scott Walker, Tom Hanks, Hulitt Gloer, Barbara Brown Taylor, Mary Earle, Lucy Hogan, Hunt Priest, Matt Zimmerman, David Boyd, Chad Vaughn, Ken Malcolm, Kevin Schubert, Zane Wilemon, Tony Baker, Charlie Cook, Roger Paynter, Cynthia Kittredge, Frank Griswold, and Rowan Williams. Thanks to all of you for your impact on my life and faith.

This research was supported by the Cathedral College of Preachers at the National Cathedral in Washington, D.C., where in the fall of 2008, I was welcomed as a Fellow of the College by Shelagh Casey Brown, Wanda Rixon, Joan Roberts, and Deryl Davis. Thanks to the College, which is on a much-lamented hiatus, for hosting me and for believing that this was a project the church needed.

It was also supported by Baylor University, which granted me the research leave in fall 2008, during which I began this book and worked on others. Thanks go to Provost Elizabeth Davis; Dean of Arts and Sciences Lee Nordt; and to my department chair, Dianna Vitanza—who have supported my research, writing, and speaking—and to my colleagues and students at Baylor.

My education at the Episcopal Theological Seminary of the Southwest in Austin, Texas, prepared me to write this book. I thank my teachers, classmates, and colleagues there, especially Cynthia Kittredge, Steve Bishop, and Ray Pickett, who taught me how to read the Bible, and Charlie Cook and Roger Paynter, who taught me how to preach.

In addition to its beginnings at the National Cathedral, this book was also written at the Texas Hill Country retreat of my friend Hulitt Gloer, for which I thank him, and at the Casa del Sol retreat center at Ghost Ranch, in Abiquiu, New Mexico, for which I thank former program head Jim Baird, Casa del Sol host/companion Carole Landess, librarian Kay Johnson, and Ghost Ranch executive director Debra Hepler. Some of my research was done during my February 2009 residence at Liverpool Hope University in Liverpool, England, where I was the guest of John Wallis and the Hope Theological Society. Thanks, John, for the gift of time and engagement.

I give thanks for the great people at Westminster John Knox, who have given me books to write that engage my mind, heart, and soul. I am grateful for my editor and editorial director, David Dobson; for wonder-editor Jana Riess, who helped me polish the book; for my publicist, Emily Kiefer; and for my editor at The Thoughtful Christian, David Maxwell. Thanks also go to the WJK staff who get these books out and into the hands of readers, and to my U.K. and European publicist Elaine Reed and the rest of the staff at Alban Books in Edinburgh, Scotland.

Finally, I give thanks for my boys, Chandler and Jake. You are the great personal joys God has given me, and I do not forget it.

Even when I seem to.

Greg Garrett
National Cathedral
Washington, D.C.
Pentecost 2010

Chapter 1

Introduction

The Problem of Contemporary Christianity

Major Ideas
1. What's wrong with American Christianity.
2. How cultural shifts affect religion.
3. How a thoughtful twenty-first-century Christianity might look.

One doesn't have to read the news (or watch it) too closely these days to begin thinking that something has gone badly wrong with American Christianity. While long-established Protestant denominations like the Presbyterian, Episcopal, and Methodist churches wrangle over questions of morality and continue to hemorrhage members (as they have done now for the past half century), the Roman Catholic Church suffers horrible harm to its reputation for covering up priestly abuse and other misconduct and now pays for it financially—and by the loss of faith among the flock. Meanwhile, some megachurches and Pentecostals continue to gain converts, but often at the cost of true engagement with the world—or even with God.

A major 2008 poll from the Pew Forum on Religion and Public Life quantifies some of the damage, which seems to be extensive: Over a fourth of Americans have left their original faith for another tradition—or for none at all; without the inflation provided by Catholic immigrants, for example, the Catholic Church in the United States would have suffered stunning losses of people who now no longer count themselves Catholic. Perhaps the most disturbing statistic for

1

the future of the church is that one in four Americans between 18 and 29 years of age claims no religious affiliation whatsoever.[1] As *The Atlantic* reports:

> Catholic and Protestant decline has coincided with the rise of the religiously unaffiliated, whose numbers have more than doubled in a decade-and-a-half. Being unaffiliated isn't necessarily the same as being an unbeliever. Many Americans who don't identify with any particular faith presumably retain spiritual beliefs of one sort or another. But what's long made America exceptional among developed nations is the strength of organized religion, and it appears that strength is weakening.[2]

More-recent polls verify this data, and the trend seems unlikely to change: among America's Buster and Mosaic generations (people aged 16–41), well over 30 million identify themselves as being "outsiders" to the Christian faith, and this number grows generationally (that is, each successive group of young people is even less likely than the one before it to be attracted to Christianity).[3] It seems to be a mass movement away from the faith as it is currently practiced. Add to the mix the fact that many observers suggest that the culture is now going through one of those mammoth periodic readjustments in the way we think, see, believe, and act—Phyllis Tickle, for example, believes that we are going through a paradigm shift that occurs once every five hundred years—and the challenge to mainstream Christian perception, belief, and practice becomes that much more apparent.[4]

In response to the terrorist attacks of 9/11, some writers and thinkers have observed that religious faith in general is too dangerous in a multifaith world, and the recent attempts to legitimize war, scientific, and policy decisions with reference to a particular strain of American Christianity has played right into the arguments of these so-called New Atheists. As Sam Harris writes in his book *The End of Faith*, "technical advances in the art of war have finally rendered our religious differences—and hence our religious *beliefs*—antithetical to our survival. We can no longer ignore the fact that billions of our neighbors believe in the metaphysics of martyrdom, or in the literal truth of the book of Revelation, or any of the other fantastical notions that have lurked in the minds of the faithful for millennia—because our neighbors are now armed with chemical, biological, and nuclear weapons."[5]

So the battle lines are drawn; critics see American Christianity as, at best, judgmental and irrelevant. At worst, it is irrational and even dangerous. And all around us, our culture and our world are going through monumental changes. How can Christianity possibly cope with these problems?

Some Christians and their traditions seek relevancy and try to accommodate the changes by adapting to the culture they see around them: think, for example, of megachurches that connect with modern audiences through an entertainment or self-help orientation, or by adopting the gated-community model of providing safety, privacy, and services to a select clientele. Others pull back entirely inside the walls, raise the drawbridge, and preach the old-time religion. Religious fundamentalism (in every faith tradition) is a common response to the fast-moving changes we are experiencing, as Karen Armstrong observes: "Much of fundamentalism is a response to this painful transformation."[6] Fundamentalists try to hold fast to the way (they think) things have always been done, to the things (they think) have always been core beliefs, even if they don't seem to be working well any more (or never have, if we are honest).

Christianity's reputation has taken what may be a well-deserved beating, although not all of this decline in respect is due merely to perceived scandal and observed contention. As I was just suggesting, it also has something to do with the kind of Christian faith represented by a vast number of American Christians. Thus my friend and former priest Greg Rickel, the Episcopal bishop of Olympia (Western Washington) told me:

> Christianity has become the institution, rather than the message. I hate to say it, but it often appears to me that those peering in from the outside know more about us than we know about ourselves. They actually do know the good things of Christianity but can't seem to find it much anymore within those who call themselves Christian. I realize that this sounds very harsh, but I think our situation demands some level of bluntness.

Well, the bishop of Olympia probably knows a few things concerning the institution—and the problems facing the church. I agree with his assessment here. Even the lives of those who identify themselves as followers of Jesus are often defined more by church attendance and a few strongly held opinions concerning personal morality than they are by a transformed life. Pollster George Barna, an evangelical who criticizes contemporary American Christianity, has done longitudinal studies pointing out that those who identify themselves as regular churchgoers do not carry their worship into their daily lives, and in fact, many do not even feel that they have connected with God during worship. Moreover, many American Christians consume, pursue, and value the same things as their secular fellows. Barna reports that few of the believers he has surveyed define success in spiritual terms. Instead, they buy into many of our secular societal myths and success stories connected to professional achievement, family, accomplishments, and financial gain. So even those who describe themselves as very religious are sometimes not actually religious, at least in terms of life-changing spiritual practice; they are just people who happen to go to church on Sunday and, say, disapprove of homosexual marriage.[7]

Biblical scholar and college professor Marcus Borg observes that half of his students who have been raised outside the Christian tradition have a "very negative stereotypical view of Christianity," finding the "most publicly visible form" of American Christianity literalistic, anti-intellectual, self-righteous, judgmental, and prejudiced.[8] Borg's anecdotal findings are borne out by more-scientific studies. In their book *unChristian*, David Kinnaman and Gabe Lyons present statistics from another longitudinal study suggesting that Christianity's reputation among young people could hardly be lower. If you have the courage to identify yourself as a Christian to young people outside the faith, then statistically speaking they are likely to think that you loathe homosexuals (as 91 percent of them believe), that you are judgmental (87 percent), and that you are hypocritical (85 percent).[9] Other perceptions from Kinnaman and Lyons's polling also sting: young people (and certainly some older ones as well) believe that Christianity is out of touch with reality, too concerned with temporal and political power, insensitive, intolerant, confusing—and boring. (And truth to tell, this is the very church I recognize from my experiences in various denominations as a child, teenager, and young adult, if not my experience in the traditions I work within now.)

Young people also say that the Jesus whom they're seeing lifted up by many American churches is not the Jesus of the Bible, but a manufactured Jesus—the Spiteful Jesus of Scott Cairns's poem at the beginning of this book—that Christians have created. So where is the Other Jesus, the one who taught and modeled love, inclusion, transformation, and a life of service? He is not to be found in many churches. Many American Christians have warped the figure of Jesus almost beyond recognition to support agendas of intolerance, imperialism, political power, and self-congratulatory salvation. These are, as Bishop Rickel says, harsh truths, but truths nonetheless. Taken together, they add up to a tremendously negative perception of a faith tradition whose founder, Jesus—as outsiders rightly understand—is supposed to have given his very life so that all of his followers might be transformed. That positive understanding seems to be all but lost as we look at the negative polling data. Why would anybody want to be a follower of Jesus, seeing the faith promoted by many churches? Or as a woman I used to date once protested when I told her I had been admitted to seminary, "Why on earth would you want to be around Christians all day?"

I myself held these same opinions for most of my life, and I held them from direct understanding of these very kinds of Christianity. As a young man, I fled from the Christian traditions in which I was raised because the faithful seemed only concerned with three things: their own souls (we, in fact, polled our souls every Sunday to ascertain if we were still really and truly saved from eternal hellfire), dictating the behavior of others (I learned, for example, that God was supremely concerned that Oklahomans might bet on horse racing, the premier moral issue in the church of my youth), and the continued growth in membership and local prestige of our particular fellowship (God's preference for your way of belief was clear if you worshiped in a bigger sanctuary than the church down the street).

I fled this and other Christian traditions I had experienced because they proved themselves to be decidedly uncompassionate when life was hard, because they had no room in their theology for thinking and creativity, because they saw everything in black and white. I also fled because I witnessed how they brutalized my mother when she and my father divorced. That moment was an opportunity for them to minister to the brokenness of my family, to be the church that heals and supports; instead, they magnified it by their judgment, hypocrisy, and bigotry toward one of the faithful who now didn't fit their norms.

I fled, in other words, because the church of my youth exactly matched the negative profile that Kinnaman and Lyons compiled in their polling some decades after my initial run-in with American Christianity: Judgmental. Hypocritical. Concerned with surface details.

And I fled to—well, to nothing. I attended church from time to time over the next few decades but never felt interested enough to invest myself in Christian life. Even when the preaching was dynamic and the music pleasant, it honestly seemed like a waste of time. Maybe it was.

So for almost twenty-five years, like many contemporary people seeking understanding, I looked for meaning outside the strictures of religious institutions; to paraphrase the title of a recent book, I liked Jesus, but I didn't like the church. I read Christian and Jewish theology and religious history. I studied Buddhist works on contemplation and mindfulness. I sought God in the mountains and in the desert. And I was fortunate enough to be loved by a few people of authentic Christian faith who did not allow me to become completely disconnected from the tradition.

But mostly I just spun in futile search for something that would give my life meaning, and like many people, I never seriously considered that Christianity would ever be that place. Like those polled by Kinnaman and Lyons, I thought I had a fairly good read on what Christianity was. I had seen the Spiteful Jesus up close and personal.

And why would I want to be around Christians all day?

Ah, but if I had only fallen in with a different kind of Christians (which I did, later, as you have probably guessed), how might things have been different? In *The Secret Message of Jesus*, my friend Brian McLaren tells a story—and I want to retell it here—about his friend Tony Campolo, a pastor and writer who was in another city late one night and couldn't sleep, so he was out having coffee in a doughnut shop. While he was there, he overheard a conversation between two prostitutes—coffee-shop regulars, it turned out—who were taking a break between tricks.

As they talked, Tony overheard that one of them, Agnes, was going to have a birthday the next day and that Agnes had never had a birthday party in her whole difficult life. So after the prostitutes went back to work, Tony enlisted the coffee-shop owner and the shop-owner's wife and launched a birthday conspiracy.

The next night—again, late—when Agnes walked inside, everyone in the coffee shop shouted, "Surprise!" and Tony and the patrons threw a birthday party for her—cake, candles, decorations, the whole deal. Agnes was blown away. After she had left—carrying her cake, which she didn't want to cut because she wanted to take it home and savor the memory—Tony led the party guests in a prayer for Agnes, and they realized for the first time that Tony was a pastor.

"What kind of church do you come from, anyway?" the shop owner asked him.

"The kind of church that throws birthday parties for prostitutes at 3:30 in the morning," Tony told him.

"No, you ain't," this guy said. "There ain't no church like that. If there were, I'd join it."[10]

I guess, based on what the coffee-shop owner had experienced of Christianity, he was expecting moral outrage, condemnation, judgment. The Spiteful Jesus. Instead, he witnessed pity, compassion, love. And it was so startling to him that he could not get his mind around it.

After the other stories we've been hearing about the church, I think this is a vital corrective, showing us what Christian faith could and should be, a story that actually sounds like something that the Other Jesus might have done. It turns us in the direction of what might become a Christian life worth living, one that—instead of filling people with anger and disgust—might inspire admiration and encourage people to belong to something larger than themselves, something with the power to change their lives and the lives of others. It suggests a Christian life rich enough to encourage 3:30 a.m. faithfulness, and loving enough to look past prejudice to locate a soul beloved by God.

So, you say, there ain't no church like that?

Maybe not.

But maybe so.

Besides the poles of accommodation and fundamentalism, leaving aside rationalism that rejects all faith, there's another viable Christian response to what futurist David Johansen describes as the volatile, uncertain, complex, and ambiguous world that has become "the new normal."[11] It is this Christian response to which I will be returning throughout this book, a Christianity that, to use Garry Wills's recent formulation, blends head and heart.[12]

What might such a Christianity look like?

How can we continue to be the people of God in this brave new world?

Well, to begin with, the challenging present calls for a faith that doesn't withdraw in fear, doesn't react or accommodate, and doesn't dumb down—or water down—belief and practice in response to either the strident truth claims of fundamentalists or the changes and challenges of this new normal. American evangelical Jim Wallis says we need to become more, not less, religious—but to substitute good religion for bad:

> Fundamentalism, it is often said, is taking religion too seriously. The answer [some think] is to take it less seriously. That conventional wisdom is wrong. The best response to fundamentalism is to take faith *more* seriously than fundamentalism sometimes does. The best response is to critique by faith the accommodations of fundamentalism to theocracy and violence and power and to assert the vital religious commitments that fundamentalists often leave out—namely compassion, social justice, peacemaking, religious pluralism, and I would say democracy as a religious commitment.[13]

Noble goals, if we can get there. Still, this is hardly the kind of faith most Americans—particularly those outside the tradition—recognize as Christian.

When, after twenty-five years of wandering, I came back to church, I finally encountered the Other Jesus. I discovered an authentic message of love and acceptance, the one that the Other Jesus seems to be exemplifying in the Christian Testament. (We also call this the New Testament; I'm using the terms interchangeably in this book because I want to suggest that the Christian [New] and Hebrew [Old] Testaments are both powerful witnesses to God, that one is not "New" and the other outdated.) I discovered believers who were trying to live lives that reflected the change this Other Jesus had wrought in them. I discovered people who practiced faith as well as preached it. In short, I discovered that many other people—the "other Christians," as Diana Butler Bass calls them—were seeking and finding the Other Jesus: the one who commanded peace, the one who served instead of grabbing power, the one who healed and fed, the one who stood against the powers and principalities of this world. This is the Jesus who—instead of the dizzying array of negative commandments promoted by many American Christians—left only one.[14] In the Gospel of John, Jesus told his followers, "I give you a new commandment, that you love one another. Just as I have loved you, you also should love one another. By this everyone will know that you are my disciples, if you have love for one another" (John 13:34–35). This way of following Christ is not concerned with an array of commandments or simply with holding the right beliefs. As we'll see, it is centered on loving each other and loving God, what Augustine called the twofold commandment of love that is at the heart of Christian faith. This love is where the rubber meets the road, where faith meets the world.

So I don't care to introduce you to the Spiteful Jesus. I'm not here to talk you into joining an exclusive club or to prep you to answer the Great Pop Quiz correctly. But I do want to talk about how a thoughtful Christianity that takes seriously the twofold commandment of love could reshape our lives, bring hope into a world filled with fear and despair, and create a powerful sense of connection with the source of truth, beauty, joy, and justice—the Creator of all that is.

Walk along with me, and let's see where the Other Jesus might lead us, what faith and practice and fellowship with the Other Christians might look like.

It's a journey that has changed my life—and saved my life, as well as my soul.

I have no doubt it could do the same for you, if it hasn't already.

For Further Discussion

1. Have you ever experienced any of the negative reactions toward (or about) people of faith that these polls suggest? Which of these conclusions about Christians seem to have some validity?
2. How many versions of American Christianity are you personally familiar with? Do you know people (friends, members of your family) whose notion of faith and practice differs markedly from yours? Where do you find common ground with them?
3. Phyllis Tickle writes that we are in the midst of a culturewide shift that is already changing everything we know and believe. Has

your own faith changed and adapted in recent years? What about the practice, worship, and mission of your faith community?
4. What does the phrase "the Other Christians" make you think of? Do you identify with this term?

For Further Reflection and Study

George Barna, *Revolution* (Carol Stream, IL: Tyndale House Publishers, 2005). Looking at shifts within the church and within culture, Barna argues for a revolution to take place in Christian belief and practice, one that will be less oriented around church membership than around a passionate commitment to God and each other.

Diana Butler Bass, *Christianity for the Rest of Us: How the Neighborhood Church Is Transforming Faith* (San Francisco: HarperOne, 2006). A groundbreaking study of mainline Protestant American churches that are thriving amid change and why they seem able to buck the trends. Individuals can learn much from this beautifully written book about what makes for a vital and adaptable Christian faith today.

David Dark, *The Sacredness of Questioning Everything* (Grand Rapids: Zondervan, 2009). Instead of arguing that Christianity is assenting to a set of core beliefs, Dark calls us to question everything and to refuse to isolate ourselves even from people and experiences that seem antithetical to ours, since God may (and indeed does) reside in them. Our salvation, in other words, may be found where we least expect it.

David Kinnaman and Gabe Lyons, *unChristian: What a New Generation Really Thinks about Christianity . . . and Why It Matters* (Grand Rapids: Baker Books, 2007). Kinnaman and Lyons report on a long-running, wide-ranging longitudinal study into attitudes toward Christianity. Small-group resources and a PowerPoint presentation are available at www.unchristian.com.

Phyllis Tickle, *The Great Emergence* (Grand Rapids: Baker Books, 2008). One of America's premier students of religion explains why the culture—including the world of faith—is in upheaval: we stand at the threshold of a seismic shift in how we live, what we do, and what we believe. Faith and belief that don't shift and grow to accommodate those changes will dry up and disappear.

Chapter 2

Faith and Belief

Major Ideas
1. What makes someone Christian.
2. The difference between belief and believing.
3. Redefining faith as relationship.

Some years ago, in the early 1990s, I met one of my heroes, Maya Angelou, a writer, civil rights activist, actress, singer, and person of faith. If you don't know Maya Angelou, go and Google her this instant: she's Oprah on multivitamins.

Ms. Angelou came to Baylor University, the fine Texas university where I have taught for the past twenty years, to give a campuswide lecture, and during her stay she did two things that I have never forgotten. First, at the banquet welcoming her to Baylor, she gently—but vocally—took us to task for the lack of diversity represented in the dining room. Although Baylor has become a more racially diverse school than even our huge public university neighbors, that night, as Ms. Angelou pointed out, the only black faces in the room—besides hers—were waiting tables. As I looked around, I saw white faculty, white administrators, and even some prize white students. It stung to recognize the truth of her observation, but I believe it has made a difference in Baylor ever since.

Second—and I blush a little to relate this, as I do every time I tell it—Ms. Angelou was invited to visit a class in the English

11

Department, and after she had finished speaking and the students were filing out, I went up to thank her for coming.

I understand, now that people say such things to me, how patronizing I was to her, how what I intended as serious praise sounded like something far less. And knowing that I intended only to compliment, I try to react with something like her grace and dignity when someone gives me a taste of my own medicine.

"Ms. Angelou," I told her, "I just wanted to tell you how grateful I am for what you've written and all you've done. I'm amazed at everything you've accomplished."

And then the shame begins. "And to think," I said, "you're a Christian."

I think what I meant by that was something like "And how great that a Christian accomplished all these things." In those days, although I would have described myself as, at best, "culturally Christian," just as some Jewish people describe themselves as cultural Jews, I didn't much like Christians. Maya Angelou restored my hope a little, as Martin Luther King did, that maybe I could be some kind of Christian someday, but my general reaction to Christianity in those days was not exactly positive.

So I'm sure that what I intended as "Thanks for giving me hope in Christianity" actually sounded like "I'm really kind of amazed that a Christian would care about any of these things, let alone do them so well."

Ms. Angelou was sitting at a desk when I went to speak to her, and she had taken my hand when I introduced myself. She still held it as she looked up at me. A gentle smile broke across her face, and she shook her head—at my question or at me or both.

"Oh, honey," she said in that deep rich resonant voice, "I am not a Christian. I am *trying* to be a Christian."

She squeezed my hand as punctuation and let it go.

Then she said her good-byes, got up, walked out of the classroom, and as far as I know, out of my life forever.

But as I heard historian Thomas Cahill say recently at Washington National Cathedral, "Acts of generosity have untold consequences," and this act of generosity may have saved my life—or at least begun that action.

Though it would be years—literally—before I could get my head around what she had offered me that day at Baylor, after a long time, after some wandering in the wilderness and thrashing in the dark places at the bottom of the sea, I realized that what she was presenting me with was a new way of believing in God, a way of questioning that didn't demand all the answers, a way of pilgrimage that didn't depend on a single moment of faith. That way could be (and has been) satisfying and life changing, a journey growing out of a decision, rather than a single decision isolated in time and space.

In *unChristian*, David Kinnaman and Gabe Lyons do more than just record all the bad things that people (and by "people," I include, possibly, you and me) have thought about Christians in recent years, as expressed in their polling data. They also draw some conclusions, one of which has to do with belief and salvation: Most people exposed to Christianity are barely getting their feet wet, since many popular ways of being Christian make Christian faith into "mere mental allegiance to a religion. The truth is that when a person makes a commitment to Christ, it is just the first step into a much-larger reality."[1] And so it should be, although it certainly starts with a commitment of some sort.

It is that larger reality that Ms. Angelou was trying to communicate to me and that I, steeped as I had been in evangelical American Christianity, could not yet get my head around.

When I was a little boy, I was taught that Christianity consisted largely of answering a certain question in the positive: "Do you believe Jesus Christ is the Son of God, the Savior of the world?"

Mere mental allegiance, if you will.

Once they had answered the question—"Have you been saved? Do you know the Lord?" or "Have you professed a belief in Jesus Christ as your personal Lord and Savior?"—in the affirmative, many Christians felt secure in their salvation and left it at that.

So Christianity has often been taught as this equation you solve for *x*. Something simple and, once solved, done. You can be saved if you read a Gospel tract and assent to its final page. There are three Bible verses, four spiritual laws, five rules of salvation, or a Sinner's Prayer.

In any case, in many Christian traditions, if you answered the question correctly and agreed to the conditions stipulated by your tradition, that was it: you were a Christian. Faith, belief, and eternal life could all be boiled down once and for all into a single question and a single answer. As long as you made that profession before you died, you were set. (I had a childhood fantasy that diverted me during many sermons: I would be a bank robber and kiss a lot of girls and accept Jesus on my deathbed after as depraved a life as the ten-year-old I was then could imagine.)

And yet, there's Ms. Angelou—may her words echo down through the ages:

"Oh, honey, I am not a Christian. I am *trying* to be a Christian."

Not just "Do you believe?" but "What do you believe?"

And "How do you believe it?"

Today, as polls like the one in *unChristian* tell us, many Americans are spiritual refugees, adrift from the traditions they once occupied, if only as an accident of birth. Some have found safe harbor and community in other faith traditions; some are happily voyaging alone; some are feeling windswept, and waves are crashing over their bows. And while a vast number of people continue to find fulfillment in a religious life marked by simple truths and onetime belief statements, for many others, that seeming tropical paradise has not been even remotely tempting.

In my own case, some years ago, after my boat had sprung leaks and I had narrowly escaped rocky waters, I pulled into a harbor where people began, rather than ended, their spiritual journeys. For me, that place was St. James Episcopal Church, an inclusive, multicultural, multiracial church in East Austin, Texas, and more recently, St. David's in downtown Austin. For writer Anne Lamott, another of my heroes (and another who thought Christianity had nothing whatsoever to offer her), it was St. Andrew's Presbyterian Church, an inclusive multicultural community in Marin City, California. Perhaps you've heard other stories or have your own connection to an unlikely group, to a community of believers you stumbled into that rescued you and started you on an authentic journey of faith.

And perhaps you are still looking.

If so, please don't stop. There are such places all over the United States, no matter where you might find yourself. For over twenty years, for example, I have taught in Waco, Texas, described by some as the Baptist Vatican. You might indeed set foot in a dozen extremely conservative Southern Baptist churches before finding a Baptist church that imagines people on a quest to work alongside God in the healing of creation. But eventually you would find yourself at Lakeshore Baptist Church, or at Seventh & James Baptist Church, or at Dayspring. And there, even there in one of the strongholds of conservative Baptist life, you could begin a spiritual journey that would be meaningful and lifelong and not revolve purely around your answering an altar call to claim your salvation once and for all.

And if you don't find the place you're looking for, you could always create your own. My friend Chris Seay started University Baptist Church in the middle of a ruined neighborhood in Waco, offering dynamic worship and a call to social justice. He has since planted Ecclesia, a church in the artsy and freewheeling Montrose district of Houston, which drills water wells in Africa and gets girls out of sexual slavery in Asia. All it takes to be a church is other people who want to worship and serve Christ.

In the various churches where I spent my childhood, I was taught that faith was static: the answers were all known, all contained in the Bible, which was God's instruction manual, and that inside the walls of the church, we were in a safe haven from a dark and dangerous world. At St. James Episcopal, though, I was taught that it was okay to ask questions, that doubt was a necessary element of faith, that we journey toward understanding individually and in community, and that I should expect eventually to patch up my battered boat and journey back out into the world rather than dwelling forever in my safe harbor.

Most important, I was taught that faith and belief are verbs, not nouns; we don't believe and sit down, content that we are saved. As Rowan Williams, the archbishop of Canterbury, puts it, once we take an initial step of trust, "the actual teaching, the doctrine, flows out of that."[2] We don't have to know everything from the start; much will be revealed on the journey. William Sloane Coffin put it this way: "I love the recklessness of faith. First you leap, and then you grow wings."[3]

We begin to believe and go right on believing, even though sometimes, given the state of things, it requires real effort.

But if we don't assent to a simple salvation equation, what do we believe?

What makes us Christian if it isn't a declaration of faith?

My rector (the priest in charge) when I walked in the back door of St. James Episcopal in Austin was Greg Rickel, the Episcopal bishop from western Washington we met in the last chapter. During my confirmation class, he taught us the basics of our faith; I discovered that there were plenty of things I'd been taught while growing up that didn't seem to matter anymore—and some things I had never been taught that mattered a great deal.

Brian McLaren has written that one of the things that turns away those seeking Jesus is that too often they are asked by the churches or denominations they enter to "swallow a lot of additional stuff"; these are things that are not essential items of faith, perhaps, but they have become so important in those traditions that they can't be separated from true orthodoxy. In Pentecostal churches, say, it might be the importance of speaking in tongues; in Baptist congregations, it might be the condemnation of dancing or alcohol; in Roman Catholic circles, it might be veneration of the saints. These are things that these Christians believe define Christianity, even if they're not necessarily accepted by other followers of Jesus as important.[4]

How do we sort these out?

What do we believe, and how?

For many people, these questions can be answered satisfactorily by the historic creeds of the church: the Nicene Creed, the Apostles' Creed, the Athanasian Creed. For many centuries these creeds have been a gathering place for Christians from various traditions and beliefs, and they remain meaningful today. Some years ago when Chris Seay and I began working on a new Bible translation for emerging Christianity, *The Voice*, we rounded up writers and scholars from all over the contemporary Christian landscape. There were people from the emerging Christian tradition like Chris and Brian McLaren; there were members of mainline Protestant churches like Lauren Winner and Phyllis Tickle and me; there were evangelical Christians; there were Roman Catholics. There were liberals, moderates, and conservatives.

And all of us were involved in putting together this enormous, costly, and quite controversial project for Thomas Nelson, the world's largest religious publisher. It's better known as the publisher of such folks as Billy Graham and Christian inspirational writer Max Lucado than as the home of cutting-edge Christianity.

I'd have to speculate that there was some nervousness at Thomas Nelson around gathering all these different birds inside one cage, and I'm sure they expected (and got) some attacks on the project because of that. To defuse charges of heresy or unorthodoxy, the publishers asked Chris and me if there was any way we could come to some basic agreements on what we, as a group, believed. I know from experience, often through interactions with people I love, that many people who call themselves Christian nonetheless seem to hold some particular beliefs that are diametrically opposed to mine.

At the *Voice* project, none of us wanted to sign some narrow statement of belief (unless, of course, it was our own narrow beliefs), but it didn't take us long to realize that we did have something we could all affirm: The Nicene Creed, something that has been repeated by Christians since the early days of the church.

The creeds are actually the formational documents of Christianity. We call them creeds because they come from the Latin word *credo*, which means "I believe" or "I give my heart to." When we say the creeds, as many Christians do in worship and in prayer, we are declaring that these are the beliefs of our hearts, that these are the beliefs that define who we are, the stories by which we understand our own stories.

The two best-known creeds, the Nicene Creed and the Apostles' Creed, go back to the very first centuries of the Christian Church, and they embody a set of beliefs that, challenging as they might be, have satisfied Christians for over fifteen hundred years. They also, as you have heard, represent a set of unifying beliefs around which Christians from different traditions can still gather, which is what they were intended to do; when the Roman emperor Constantine convened the Council of Nicaea in AD 325, the gathered Catholic bishops put together a set of beliefs that the majority of them could assent to; a later version, the one we say now, emerged from a similar council of bishops.

Although we'll explore them in our next chapter, at their heart, what the historic creeds do is tell a story about God's desire for us and how we understand and experience God: We say that we believe in one God, the God who created the universe, whom we experience as the Father. We say that we believe that Jesus, who was called the Christ, the Anointed One, was his Son—sent to earth in human form to pursue us and draw us back into close relationship with God. We say that we believe that a Spirit, a third manifestation of God, was sent to comfort and instruct us. That's it as far as what Christians agree in the creeds to believe about God, but it seems to be enough; it seems to open the door for people to approach this story as they can and will.

Some people believe every word of the historic creeds literally; some approach them as a narrative that they believe whether or not they are literal fact; some say them as a regular profession of faith: these are the things I want to believe. In each case where people believe them with their hearts, however they understand them with their heads, they are professing their faith in God, and in Jesus as the one who is their path to God.

That's not to say that some people don't have trouble saying the creeds. In one of his many books, the liberal Episcopal bishop John Shelby Spong wrote that he had difficulty in saying the creeds because they contain so many supernatural elements, so many frankly unbelievable things. (I myself used to mumble parts of the creed that I couldn't yet accept in my heart, although now I speak out strong and clear.) Ultimately the creeds seem to be less concerned with what is believable and more concerned with what I want to believe. The writer Kathleen Norris tells a story in her book *Amazing Grace* about a seminarian and a Greek Orthodox priest who seem to think of the creeds in opposing ways. The seminarian keeps asking the priest, "How am I supposed to say the creeds if I don't believe them?"

And every time he asks, the priest just says, "Keep saying them and you will believe them."[5]

In twelve-step spirituality there's a like understanding—"Fake it until you make it"—and a Christian version of this comes from Ignatius of Loyola: "Act as if you have faith, and faith will be given to you."

But in each case, I think it's important to know that people don't consider faith to be settled once and for all; rather, you "do" faith, you work at it, you try to understand what you believe and why.

I am *trying* to be a Christian.

That's part of the journey, and part of why—for what we're calling here "the other Christians"—a little doubt, a few hard questions, or even a big I-don't-get-it are not deal breakers. It's not all about assent; it *is* all about intent.

And it's also important to recognize that faith is often a challenge and sometimes difficult. The Bible is filled with contradictions: different portraits of God that seem hard to hold together, verses—or entire books—of the Bible that seem to stand in tension with each other. There are historical and cultural elements in the Bible that frighten and disturb us, such as the violence, the cultural chauvinism, the disrespect toward women.

Yet, as we'll discuss in a later chapter, there is a clear message that emerges from this tangle of stories: The Bible tells us that there is a God of creative love who desires a relationship with human beings, a God who is willing to forgive our mistakes, failures, and rebellion if we will only turn to God.

For many American Christians, this relationship is often transactional: If I believe what I'm supposed to believe, then God will do things for me in return. Even some progressive Christians fall into this trap, although for us it's often less about "orthodoxy" (believing the right thing) then it is about "orthopraxy" (*doing* the right thing). In either case, though, it becomes a matter of false belief.

Let's be straight on something that is true regardless of which transaction we believe in: If God is truly God—that is, the Creator and Ruler of the universe and all that—then we owe God everything. And God owes us nothing. God created us. God sustains our lives. God has told us that we can choose to have fullness of life in relationship and service.

To imagine that either by your belief or your actions you can induce the great power of the universe to act in a certain way is not faith: it's magic. So whether it's a megachurch pastor saying that if you believe hard enough or give enough, God will make you rich; or a Christian social justice advocate saying that if you do the right thing for others, God will do the right thing for you—any belief that we control or with which we influence God is equally flawed.

What God gives us—chooses of God's own free will to give us—is love, and the sense of God's presence in all times, good and bad. What God offers us is relationship, and that is pure grace, certainly more than we deserve.

When I first started working on this book, one day I was in Union Station in Washington, D.C., people watching while I waited for my train. A young couple caught my eye—a handsome young soldier and his beautiful girl in a red dress were walking hand in hand—when suddenly they turned, twirled, and were dancing under the vaulted ceiling. As they danced, they looked at each other, whispered to each other, and laughed. In that moment, I believe they were totally and completely alive.

God has created us for relationship with him, as the Genesis story of Adam and Eve first tells us. It's almost impossible to take this story literally as an account of the two first human beings, but we can take it seriously as a story of how God seeks to be in relationship with us—and seeks our obedience and acquiescence.

But we have to be willing to give ourselves to the dance.

If the girl loves her soldier, she will not force him to love her—in fact, since he has been created with opinions and free will, she cannot force him. She can only trust that if he loves her as she loves him, that he will tell her—and show her—by taking her hand, by stepping out onto the dance floor.

Our relationship with God operates in similar fashion. God's hand is extended to us from before our ability to respond to it. God has always loved us. And God will go on loving us, even if we do not take God's hand and step out on the dance floor, even if we do not choose to love God back. But if we do choose this, we enter into the fullness of life and experience all that God has planned for us.

It is by thinking of belief as relationship—rather than belief as an exam we must pass—that we enter into true life with God. It isn't enough, the Bible tells us, to believe in God. One can believe in God without having a relationship with him, and Jesus tells us in the Gospel of Matthew that when judgment comes, many people will say they believe in Jesus, although they don't honestly know him at all: "'It is not anyone who says to me, 'Lord, Lord,' who will enter the kingdom of Heaven," Jesus tells us, "but the person who does the will of my Father in heaven" (Matthew 7:21 NJB).

The Gospel of Matthew goes still further; throughout its pages it tells us that belief is not enough, that what we must be doing is what Jesus teaches us to do. Belief should change us. The Greek word *metanoia* is often translated in the Bible as "repentance," a word that has taken on all kinds of unpleasantness from its use by hellfire-and-brimstone preachers and accusatory Christians. I want to reclaim it for our twenty-first-century Christianity, since what it truly means is *transformation*, the sense of turning your life around, of becoming an entirely new person.

When you believe, or begin to believe, it should take you from the path you were on and plant your feet on a new one.

Not yet at a destination, of course.

But on the way.

For Further Discussion

1. What is your own understanding of what and how we believe in God? Has your conception changed over your lifetime?
2. How would the idea of pilgrimage differ from the mainstream idea of the profession of faith? What does each idea offer?
3. The author writes that we should not expect God to do what we want. How does this differ from some understandings of religion? Why do we pray if not to get what we want?
4. Can you remember a time when you or someone you know changed for the better? What caused that change?

For Further Reflection and Study

Barbara Brown Taylor, *Leaving Church: A Memoir of Faith* (San Francisco: Harper-SanFrancisco, 2006). In this personal account of her journey of faith, Taylor recounts her transition from priest to professor, from someone who experienced God primarily within the church to one who found God all around her.

Paula Huston, *By Way of Grace: Moving from Faithfulness to Holiness* (Chicago: Loyola Press, 2007). In this book about faith translated into virtues, Huston explores transformative Christian faith and practice by focusing on the cardinal virtues of the faith as exemplified by different saints.

Brian McLaren, *A Generous Orthodoxy* (Grand Rapids: Zondervan, 2004). McLaren explores the variety of ways Christians have believed, arguing that each offers something of value, that too many artificial distinctives are introduced alongside real doctrine, and that belief not put into action is dead.

Rowan Williams, *Tokens of Trust: An Introduction to Christian Belief* (Louisville, KY: Westminster John Knox Press, 2007). The archbishop of Canterbury introduces the most important elements of Christian faith by taking readers on a guided tour of the great creeds. The central idea: God is worthy of our trust.

Chapter 3

God

Creator, Redeemer, Sustainer

> **Major Ideas**
> 1. How Christians seek to understand God.
> 2. Explaining the Trinity.
> 3. What the Trinity teaches us about relationship with God.

When I stand up in a pulpit to preach, I always ask everyone in the congregation to pray with me before we begin, and this is the prayer I use: "Holy One: Creator, Redeemer, Sustainer. Draw our hearts and minds ever closer to you, we pray."

Creator, Redeemer, Sustainer?

Didn't I just say Holy "One"?

Honestly, why don't I just say "God" and be done with it?

In classical Christian understanding, as perplexing as it might initially seem, when we pray, we are praying to a single God—a single God we experience in three persons, normally identified as God the Father, God the Son, and God the Holy Spirit.

So is it three or is it one?

Or both?

And what is up with that?

The concept of Trinity has been hurting people's heads for centuries: not only do our Scriptures seem to refer to God in different ways, but there also is this whole question of what to do about Jesus. The early church grappled with one primary theological issue: Who is Jesus? Coming, as Christianity did, out of the Jewish tradition, they felt they had a better handle on God the Father: the God of Abraham and Sarah, the God of the exodus from Egypt, the God of deliverance in the Hebrew Bible. Admittedly, God was perplexing: was this a loving God, an angry God, a militant God, a missing God? But the Hebrew Scriptures suggested that God could be approached, and even if not understood, we at least could enter into relationship with God in ways that would be meaningful.

There was also a long tradition of talking about the Spirit of God, which is said in Genesis to have moved over the deep waters in creation. The Spirit was thought to have inhabited the Holy of Holies within the Jerusalem Temple and was believed to have inspired (a word directly derived from "spirit") the messages of the Hebrew prophets. Spirit was not an alien or unknown concept to them either.

No, Jesus was the wild card in the first centuries of the Christian church, just as people today struggle with his identity: Was Jesus a prophet? A rabbi or teacher of spiritual truths? Or was he, as he and the church claim, the Christ, God's chosen one, sent to redeem the world?

And if he is the redeemer—known in Jewish tradition as the Messiah, the Anointed One, or the liberating King—then what is his relationship to God the Father? If we say he is a son, is he inferior to God, a creation? If we call him "God the Son," is he equal to God, an extension of God?

Those questions—what in theological terms we call discussion of Christology—led to a great deal of strife in the early centuries of the Christian church. In fact, they led to the Roman emperor Constantine calling the Council of Nicaea (birthplace of the Nicene Creed) in the first place. The creeds—the Nicene Creed, the Apostles' Creed, and another major creedal statement on the substance of Jesus, the Athanasian Creed—all express important doctrines concerning Jesus and his relationship to God the Father. The result, as you probably know, was the formulation of the doctrine of the Trinity, the idea that the relationship between Father, Son, and Spirit makes up the fullness of God as we understand God in Christian belief. The creeds tell us that these persons are all part of the same essence and partake of the same substance of godhood.

So we speak of one God in three persons: Creator, Redeemer, Sustainer.

But our typical way of thinking of this has often been a little off-putting; the classical notion of the Trinity formulated by Augustine and Thomas Aquinas, two of the greatest Christian theologians, separates them and their actions, as Jürgen Moltmann summarizes: they "saw the 'Father' in the divine subject of understanding and will, the 'Son' in the Word that proceeds from his understanding, and the 'Holy Spirit' in the love which proceeds from his understanding and his will."[1] And although they are beautiful expressions of the Divine, the creedal statements seem to reflect that understanding of the action of the Three-Personed God as mostly separate: "We believe in one God, the Father. . . . We believe in one Lord, Jesus Christ, the only Son of God. . . . We believe in the Holy Spirit, . . . who proceeds from the Father and the Son, and with them is worshiped and glorified." We might almost imagine a heavenly table where the three Persons of God sit around after lunch until Jesus checks his watch and says, "Oh, man, it's time to do some redeeming," and the Spirit yawns, stretches, and says, "Well, I have some comforting to do anyway. I'll see you two at dinner."

Contemporary understandings of the Trinity (and yes, people are still arguing over this) tend to be more synthetic than analytical and reflect the idea that the work that God does—*all* of the work—is done in divine community. Instead of imagining three persons sitting around a table, some contemporary theologians have encouraged us to imagine the Trinity as a dance with three participants who blend into one, and that this beautiful swirling blur, too fast or complex for our eyes to follow, is God in action, doing all the work of God: creation, redemption, sustaining life and hope and joy. This beautiful dance of the Trinity is called *perichōrēsis*, and dance is a wonderful model for how a triune God might operate as what Moltmann calls a "triunity."[2]

Music also illustrates how we might understand this triunity; theologian Jeremy Begbie often illustrates the concept of the Trinity by playing a chord. On their own, each note sounds, each note has a clarity and beauty. But together, they have something more, a perfection that individually they do not possess. We can name the individual notes, however—A, C, E, let's say—and the creeds do name the individual persons of God as a way for us to approach a deeper understanding of God. So let's see if we can simultaneously hold in our minds the image of the beautiful communal dance of the Trinity called perichoresis, and turn briefly to consider some of the historical understandings of God we can gain when we consider each of the persons individually.

We sometimes imagine God the Father as a bearded white guy on a throne somewhere—perhaps some strange combination of Zeus and Santa Claus—looking down on earth and preparing to zap or reward people based on their behavior. Any image that we have of God the Father, though—including the idea of God as Father—is anthropocentric (seen through the lens of our own human experience). God is neither male nor female; in fact, although we're told in Genesis 1:26 that God has created human beings in *our* (note the plural) image, God's true essence remains beyond our comprehension.

The classical vision of God we have from Thomas Aquinas, Anselm of Canterbury, Gregory of Nyssa, and others is that the transcendent and incorruptible essence of God cannot be caged by our language, although we can describe actions of God or natures of God. Barbara Brown Taylor summarizes these notions beautifully in a contemporary sermon: "God does not conform to our expectations. We glimpse our own relative size in the universe and see that no human being can say who God should be or how God should act. . . . We find out what is not true and are set free to seek what is."[3] God is bigger than any box into which we might seek to put God.

These voices from the tradition also tell us that God the Father Almighty is the Creator of heaven and earth; our understanding is that God existed before anything was created, and that God will go on eternally. God is that which Is, perfect Being, and the fount of all things. Thomas Aquinas wrote that "God is essential being, whereas other beings are beings by participation."[4] Everything, that is, comes from God, and God does not require anything other than God; God is perfect and complete.

But God's action as Creator—abetted by the Son (the Word that spoke creation into being) and the Spirit (breathing life into creation and maintaining it)—expresses one of the fundamental truths we profess concerning God. God created. But why? Not for any of the reasons we might imagine doing it if it were up to us. God was not lonely; the Trinity has always been, so God was in perfect community long before any other community existed. God did not lack anything; if, as Aquinas and other classical theologians have argued, God is perfect being, then to be complete, God certainly does not need a sunset or a blue whale, let alone a Harley or an iPhone.

No, our understanding of creation is that God created other beings to share the love experienced within the Trinity. Theologian Kathryn Tanner writes, "The triune God brings about a variety of different connections or union with the non-divine, for the sake of perfecting what is united with God, in an effort to repeat the perfection of God's own triune life."[5] In other words, God created (and is continuously creating) the world because God loves (and continues to love), and that love is extended to us, God's creations, without reservation, if only we will accept it.

In the book of Genesis, God reaches out to a desert tribesman named Abram and offers him a covenant—a relationship. If Abram—later to be called Abraham—would do what God asked and return his love faithfully, God would take Abraham's descendants and make them a great nation, specially favored and a sign of God's love and power. This nation became the Hebrew people, or the Jews, and this first covenant with Abraham was an example of God reaching out to his creation in love.

Remember the soldier and his girl in Union Station, who danced to music that only they could hear? Now imagine them reaching out to us to join them and promising that if we step out to dance with them, we will experience the love they feel—and hear the music they hear.

The role of Jesus, the Son, grows out of this understanding of God's desire to reach out to the creation, to express God's love for it, and to invite creation to love God in return. Jesus, in the story of God's love for us, is the Redeemer, what the Jewish people called (and still call) the Messiah. In the writings of the Hebrew Bible (which many Christians call the Old Testament), the Jewish people were told that someday God would send them a redeemer, a messiah, who would come to them and save them. After some few years of political power, wealth, and comfort, the Jews had suffered one setback after another, been conquered by one empire after another. They expected a political messiah, and many of Jesus' followers could not understand why he did not want to drive out the Roman government, the latest empire to occupy Palestine. It became clear, though, that Jesus saw himself as a different kind of messiah, called by God to preach and teach the coming kingdom of God, to heal and serve, and to suffer and die, not to fight and destroy, even on behalf of the people whom God had chosen as his special ones.

The challenge comes when we remember that Christians believe Jesus was God, but that he was also fully human. Jesus of Nazareth, this man who came into being as the son of Mary of Galilee, was a poor working Jew who followed the faith of his mother and earthly father, and who lived in Galilee, a Palestinian region ruled by a Roman occupation government. In what at the time was a cruel irony (and became simply cruel for generations of Jews persecuted by Christians because of it), Jesus was crucified by the Roman government at the direct instigation of Jewish leaders, who feared that Jesus might destabilize a political situation that was already perilous with his talk of the coming kingdom, his healing miracles, and his popular support.

In this as in many other things during his human experience, Jesus was not seen to be exceptional. Other so-called messiahs had met similar fates, and thousands of Jews were crucified by the Romans; at the time and for some years after, the cross did not signify anything except a shameful political execution.[6] Today, of course, it has come to represent almost exclusively the death and miraculous resurrection of Jesus, the *Christ* (from the Greek *Christos*, "anointed one of God"; "Christ" is not Jesus' last name but a title denoting his holiness and position). Through his death on the cross and resurrection, Jesus somehow brought all human beings into the special relationship with God that had been held solely by the Jewish people. That is, through Jesus' voluntary death in obedience to God's plan, and God's vindication of Jesus by raising him from the dead, we have all become chosen people, if we choose to accept it.

This resurrection—the supernatural, larger-than-life story that is at the beating heart of Christianity—does represent a sticking point for some people who would prefer that their faith be wholly rational. Another such difficulty is the virgin birth of Jesus. Christians believe that Jesus was conceived by the power of the Holy Spirit—that is, that he had a heavenly Father and a human mother, Mary of Galilee. This notion of divine generation is familiar to many from mythology—Zeus was always falling in love with this nymph or that cow, and hijinks ensued—but God's approach to Mary was very different, we are told. First, it was not to gratify God's lusts (unlike the Greek or Roman gods, who are actually just outsized and oversexed humans, God has no lusts to gratify); second, it was not against Mary's will, as many of the mythological "seductions" were said to be. Mary was offered a choice. The encounter we call the annunciation represents the moment when the angel Gabriel announced to Mary what God wanted to do, that with her help, God was ready to bring salvation to the world. The annunciation—God's proposal and Mary's response, "Here am I, the servant of the Lord; let it be with me according to your word"—represents the ongoing model for God's interaction with us: God reaches out, Mary reaches back, and salvation comes as a result (Luke 1:38).

Although we'll talk more about this issue in our next chapter discussing the Bible, it's important to recognize that Christians see these two supremely miraculous events in the life of Jesus—the birth and the resurrection—in different ways. For some, they are literal and historical truths; others regard them as metaphorical truths; others have left their options open but say that the stories are beautiful and ought to be true, even if they aren't. In the creeds, we say we believe these things about Jesus, not in the same way that we say that we believe that aluminum is the most abundant metal in the earth's crust—something that can be scientifically proved—but as we said in the last chapter, we say that we assent to these beliefs. We give our heart to them. We find our truth in them.

Some years ago I realized that I could never know whether the virgin birth or the resurrection were truthful events—I wasn't there, after all—but I decided to leave my mind open and to let people know that my faith in God did not depend on the historical truth, but the story truth: *This is the story I am choosing to believe because it helps me make sense of the world—and of the God I believe created it.* I believe the message of the story is more important than whether it can be verified. And I believe, with Rowan Williams, that to get too caught up in these other questions can actually have the effect of making us forget why these stories matter so much as a vision of God's movement in the world.[7]

The life-giving work of the Spirit, who conceives Jesus, the Son of God, shows us the final piece of the triune God. Spirit comes from the Latin *spiritus*, which may also be translated as "wind" or "breath," and in Latin (and in Greek and Hebrew, two other languages in which the Bible and its ideas have been transmitted), the word could conceivably be translated as any of the three. Thus wind, spirit, and breath are intimately linked, all of them invisible but powerful, and our understanding of the Spirit of God should incorporate the idea of God's breath blowing across creation (and into our lungs, as God breathed life into Adam, that first human in one of the creation stories in the book of Genesis).

In the New Testament, the Gospels show us the Spirit descending upon Jesus at his symbolic baptism at the Jordan River, at the hands of the prophet John; some believe that this moment of the Spirit's touch is the moment when Jesus truly became the Christ, the one empowered by God to miraculously heal and feed the needy, to preach the good news that God's kingdom was coming near. We find more information on the Spirit in the Gospel of John, where Jesus tells his followers that after his death and resurrection, God will send a comforter and advocate so that we can know God's continuing presence even though Jesus—God's stand-in in human form—is leaving the earthly stage. In the book of Acts, we see followers of Jesus who are given the power to speak different languages by the Spirit. The Spirit is also considered to be the power that is gathering the church together; Paul's Second Letter to the Corinthians illustrates this in its Trinitarian benediction: "The grace of the Lord Jesus Christ, the love of God, and the communion of the Holy Spirit be with all of you" (2 Corinthians 13:13). The Spirit is the bond of love drawing followers of Christ together in support and for mission. In all of these aspects, we see the Spirit's moving in the world, serving as God's presence, continually showing God's power to redeem and love.

These three understandings of God—as Creator, Redeemer, Sustainer—all tell us something of the story we inhabit: that a creator God loves us and seeks relationship with us so that God can share the joy and beauty of what God is. In the three persons of God—and because of the beautiful dance of the Trinity, the so-called perichoresis—we are invited to join in love and praise for that God who is greater than we can understand.

But that same God has helped us to understand what we need to understand—that we are invited to dance.

Where is that invitation? And how do we read it once we have found it? Well, in my faith community, we say that we understand God through Scripture, reason, and tradition, with the Bible being at the forefront of those elements. Even now when the Bible has been picked and pawed over by those who want to use it for their own purposes, it remains the primary way through which people of faith understand God and our relationship to God. In the next chapter, we'll try to understand how contemporary believers might take the Bible seriously as part of a thoughtful Christianity, even after so many years of it being read and taught so badly.

For Further Discussion

1. Does the doctrine of the Trinity make any difference in your daily faith? When you pray, do you have a distinct divine person to whom you pray? Why?
2. How does the notion of God the Father help you make connections to God? In what ways does it hinder you? Are there other ways you could name this aspect of God that would be meaningful for you?
3. What are the central elements of the story of Jesus for you? How important are his birth, life, death, or resurrection? How would you explain them to someone who wanted to know what you believe?
4. If you had to boil down your understanding of God into a few sentences, what would they be?

For Further Reflection and Study

Jack Miles, *Christ: A Crisis in the Life of God* (New York: Alfred A. Knopf, 2001). In this work (and the earlier, Pulitzer-winning *God: A Biography*), Miles describes the character of God, treating him as a literary as well as a theological figure. Jesus represents God's attempt to retell his story in new terms.

Jürgen Moltmann, *The Spirit of Life: A Universal Affirmation* (Minneapolis: Fortress Press, 2001). One of Christianity's greatest contemporary theologians returns to his long-running discussion of the Spirit of God, the member of the Trinity that seems to cause people the most difficulty. He argues that the Spirit is central to Christian life and work.

Kathryn Tanner, *Jesus, Humanity and the Trinity: A Brief Systematic Theology* (Minneapolis: Augsburg Fortress, 2001). Tanner describes the way that the Trinity is involved in creation, salvation, and the fulfillment of all God's purposes. The Trinity offers humans more opportunities for divine connection as God strives to bring all of creation toward the perfection that is God.

N. T. Wright, *Simply Christian: Why Christianity Makes Sense* (San Francisco: HarperOne, 2006). Wright explores some of the core Christian beliefs, including chapters on God the Father, Jesus and his role in the salvation of the world, and the Spirit.

Chapter 4

The Bible and Theology

Major Ideas
1. What the Bible is—and isn't.
2. How we read the Bible.
3. Why theology is essential to every believer.

*I*n the fall of 2008, I was flipping through channels after a hard day's work on this book at the National Cathedral in Washington, D.C. Sports, politics, politics, politics—the 2008 election season was coming to a close. At last I ran across Pastor John Hagee (to my simultaneous delight and chagrin, a fellow Texan) preaching on the 2008 presidential election, an event that was fitting fairly neatly into his own opinions concerning the imminent approach of the end of the world. As he preached, for each bullet point, as it were, a Scripture reference flashed onto the screen, identifying the Bible chapter and verse he was referencing. It was a prodigious display; like many evangelical Christians, he knew a ton of Bible verses and could order them forward like soldiers on the advance.

It was a typical—if dazzling—American Christian use of the Bible: the Bible is straightforward, it means what it says, it says what it means. It's God's instruction manual.

As you can see, I know what it means, since I'm citing chapter and verse.

And if, somehow, you don't agree with the way I'm using the Bible?

Then, Sister or Brother, at best, you are just flat wrong.

And at worst, you are damned for all eternity.

Many American Christians do treat the Bible as though it's a cookbook, rule book, or divine self-help guide that we only have to open and look inside and all will be obvious to us. But what all this ignores, as you're probably aware if you're taking the trouble to read this book, is that the Bible is actually damnably hard to read. I've read it front to back; I know that it's not nearly as clear as people sometimes make it out to be.

People sometimes use the Bible to prove the existence of God (which seems to me a little circular), but Rowan Williams observes that the Bible advances no systematic arguments for the existence of God; instead, it shows us moments of conflict with God, times of doubt and difficulty. "Don't imagine that the Bible is full of comfortable and reassuring things about the life of belief and trust," Williams says. "It isn't."[1] That certainly fits my experience of forty-plus years of trying to read the Bible. It is not a systematic approach to faith, although we find much concerning the life of faith within it.

Another part of our difficulty in reading the Bible is that even the people who say that the Bible is easily understood seem to have understood it in different ways at different times, making it hard to know how we're supposed to interpret it now. For example, if the Bible says that slavery is a fact of life (and the Bible's normative understanding of slavery in both the Hebrew and Christian Testaments was used to justify slavery in the eighteenth and nineteenth centuries, as entire American Christian denominations split into northern and southern units over the issue), then why isn't it okay to have slaves now?

If at various places the Bible calls for forgiveness of debts and realignment of wealth (the Hebrew Bible actually calls for a Year of Jubilee, a regular occasion when debts would be forgiven; when Jesus makes his first public appearance in the Gospel of Luke, as we will see, he reads that Scripture aloud and announces that the time of forgiveness has come), then why do we insist that such ideas are un-American or unrealistic today?

If a section of the Bible that actually does have rules and regulations prohibits the eating of pork in one place and forbids men having sex with men in another, why do some Christians happily enjoy Easter ham at the same time that they enforce a gay-free table?

When we see the tangled history of interpretation of the Scriptures, it becomes clear that the Bible isn't a rule book or a Christian Boy Scout Guide. Instead, as Scot McKnight has observed, the Bible is a book requiring our active involvement and discernment in reading and interpreting it, since, if we're brutally honest, we have to admit that all Christians—even those who claim to read the Bible literally and live out every part of it—do that only with the sections that seem most relevant to them, adapting them to fit the culture in which they belong.[2]

It might make you feel better—less challenged, if you've ever gotten bogged down in the Scriptures—to learn that the Bible is not an easily followed rule book that explains itself as it goes along. Instead, it is a library of individual books (the word "Bible" comes from the Greek *biblia*, meaning "books") written over a substantial period of time, and recording history, poetry, wisdom, and prophecy as well as the odd (sometimes very odd) rule, regulation, and request. These books are in conversation with each other and sometimes even in conflict with each other: the Letters of Paul exalt faith over any works we might perform; the Letter of James says that faith without works is dead. And from testament to testament, there is either disagreement or a growing revelation of God and God's purposes.

In the Hebrew Bible, in the books of Exodus, Joshua, Judges, and other works recording the history of God's people, God is a militant, violent, and angry deity; he strikes down armies and nations that oppose his chosen people, as well as persons within the people of Israel who disobey or dishonor him. Yet in the Christian Testament, the God of justice and mercy seems, all of a sudden, to have become a God of love, and we know this because of Jesus.

Bono, perhaps the world's most famous contemporary theologian, often says that it's through his study of the life of Jesus that he learns who God is. In that life, Jesus preached love, tolerance, acceptance, and a message of redemption that extended beyond the Jews to the Gentiles (non-Jews). His message would eventually be adopted by the apostle Paul, the most influential Christian ever.

So the early books of the Bible say that God has chosen a particular people (the Jews, the descendants of Abraham, Isaac, and Jacob), while later books, after some soul-searching, proclaim that God wants to choose everybody (which is, you have to admit, a radical shift in the course of a few hundred pages).

How are we supposed to read a book literally when different parts say such different things?

And how can anybody claim that such a book is transparent, easy to read and follow, and that it speaks clearly to anyone who will simply pick it up and read it?

Our problems come, as Marcus Borg has understood, precisely when we try to read the Bible in a simplistic or literal way; Borg's apposite statement is that we should take the Bible *seriously* but not *literally*. It is not a rule book, or the definitive guide to who is in and who is out, despite its being treated in such a way by pastors and priests for hundreds of years. It is, however, a set of writings that hold peculiar relevance for people of faith—authority, even, if we can consider how an ancient book might be considered to have authority over people living in the twenty-first century.

What is authority? Some Christians (although not I) would describe it in this way: authority controls what is permissible for us to believe; it is authority in the sense that a traffic cop represents authority. Others would say that authority is how we understand what God is trying to say to us—how the ultimate authority (God) expresses God's self.

Authority in the church has generally been understood to come from the Scriptures, from the teachings of religious traditions, and from our own reason (think Bible, pope, and scholarship as a historical way of making sense of these). In the twentieth century, especially, these were joined by a fourth method, individual revelation through thoughts and feelings that are assumed to come directly from God. Though individual Christian traditions weigh these differently, most agree that the Scriptures should be paramount; the Bible is our first, best guide to who God is and how we are supposed to relate to him, for it is in the Scriptures that we meet Jesus, God's truest revelation of self to humanity.

If we think of authority as being the range of acceptable belief—if you believe this, you are "saved"; if you don't believe this, you are damned to hell, whatever that is—then the Bible, as used by many Christians, becomes a book we open so that we can find the right answers to hard questions. It tells us what to do. It is a traffic cop, a tough-love book with a heart of gold that only wants us to do the right thing. Not all of us who read the Bible, however, agree on what those right things are. Is the right thing individual salvation? Is the right thing healing the world? Are the things we shouldn't do if we want to go to heaven the things that matter?

What this interpretive approach also ignores is that any authority that might be present in the Bible is delegated from God. All authority ultimately rests in God, and I, for one, have problems with considering the Bible "Holy" since that encourages some people to venerate the Bible rather than the God it is supposed to record and reflect. All of these forms of revelation should be in balance with each other, even if we consider Scripture to be the most important kind of revelation.

Think of this balance among forms of revelation as being like the balance of powers among the American branches of government: When any branch goes unchecked, it takes too much power for itself, which creates a dangerous imbalance that cannot easily be corrected. So it is with any of the forms of revelation. The Bible is vital to our understanding of God, but the Bible is also mediated to us through religious traditions, through our own reason and that of others, and through the guiding of the Spirit. If the Bible becomes the only object of revelation, it can become an idol; on the opposite end of the spectrum, so too might individual revelation in traditions that, for example, place the gifts of tongues or other charismatic practices on a pedestal.

Bible scholar N. T. Wright (who was also, until recently, the Anglican bishop of Durham, U.K.) is a favorite among evangelicals because he argues for the authenticity of the supernatural events recorded in the Bible; however, he is also beloved by progressive Christians because he approaches the Bible with rigor and a willingness to ask hard questions. He is certainly one of my favorite Bible scholars. Bishop Wright argues that when we assume that it is possible to just "read the text," we are ignoring the fact that we all come to the Bible with interpretive filters, whether as progressive politics or evangelical theology. "Evangelicals," Wright notes, "often use the phrase 'authority of scripture' when they mean the authority of evangelical, or Protestant, theology. . . . If we are not careful, the phrase 'authority of scripture' can . . . come to mean simply, 'the authority of the evangelical tradition.'"[3] In other words, many evangelicals who argue that the Bible is simple and straightforward find it to be that way only because they already know what they want it to say.

Albert Schweitzer observed, many years ago, that we always seem to find exactly the Jesus we are looking for.

In the five hundred years since the Protestant Reformation, the question of authority has foregrounded Scripture. In response to the pronouncements of an increasingly powerful and dogmatic Roman Catholic Church, Martin Luther called for a reliance on *sola scriptura*—only Scripture. It seemed to work for many people for hundreds of years, although for the past hundred or more it has become a greater and greater problem to take simple readings of a work written thousands of years ago and reconcile them to modern life. Today the possibility of our relying solely on Scripture has almost died out. Religious fundamentalism in America may be simply a dying gasp as people try desperately to hold on to *sola scriptura*; as Phyllis Tickle has been telling people around the country in the past few years, disputes over slavery, civil rights, and equal rights for women and gays have frayed *sola scriptura* to the breaking point. If a reliance on the "simple reading" of the Bible is no longer intellectually possible, she asks, "where now is your authority?"[4] Where indeed?

Thank goodness that literal "simple reading" is not the only way to read the Bible, and that our understanding of Scripture's authority in the life of the Christian does not (or at least should not) depend on its being a simplistic rule book. Let's return to Borg's notion that we might take the Bible seriously but not literally and ask the important question first: Should we take the Bible seriously?

I don't mean to be sacrilegious in posing this question. But if we are asking questions about the Bible, let's start with the most pertinent one: Why should we treat a disparate library of ancient writings from a vastly different culture as a work that in some way deserves our serious thought, let alone a lifetime of study and reflection? I can't think of any other written works that are two thousand or more years old that we hold up as a model for how we should live in the twenty-first century. So why these texts?

Over the years, people have answered this question differently. Some have said, "This is written by God himself," as if God dictated to a series of human stenographers in much the same way that Muslims believe that Muhammad was given the Qur'an. Well, modern historical criticism indicates that if God was dictating, he was often doing so over a period of many years to a number of editors; the

Bible shows clear evidence of having been woven together by various people, some of whom had radically different viewpoints about the material. When we add, again, the problem that individual books and verses of the Bible repeat or even directly contradict each other, then we are forced to admit that God has given us what seems to some a hopelessly bollixed-up volume. If God the Most High were dictating a message to us that he wanted us to follow without question, wouldn't he have given us something a little more, oh, I don't know, straightforward? Wouldn't he have smoothed out the contradictions, maybe written little numbers in the margins—as we imagine he does when he wants to be clear and unambiguous, as with Charlton Heston and those stone tablets? Even human writers—I think here of the modernist poet T. S. Eliot—have included footnotes or given interviews when they feared that their work might be misunderstood.

No, I think I have to side with Martyn Percy, the principal of Ripon Cuddesdon College in Oxford, who was quoted by Dan Brown in *The Da Vinci Code* as saying that God does not employ a fax machine; the Bible cannot be read as a text message from God. Greg Rickel chimes in, "I have always believed [the Bible] to be the Word of God, but certainly not the words of God," and perhaps this is a useful way for us to approach the Bible. We can agree that the Bible is, somehow, authoritative for Christian communities—agree that this is, somehow, the Word of God—but we will have to think of some reason to take the Bible seriously other than assuming that the Bible was e-mailed from God's PowerBook.

Others say the Bible is authoritative because it presents a true record of important events in the salvation narrative God has given us. But can we know that the Bible is true, in a historical sense? Despite all the expeditions to find the ark of Noah—or the ark of the covenant—despite 150 years of biblical archaeology, we still sometimes find disconnects between what the Bible says and what the record on the ground indicates. The book of Joshua claims that Joshua fought the battle of Jericho, but the archaeological record of the "city" of Jericho doesn't quite prove such a thing. Is that really a problem? Only if we're reading the Bible while expecting something we can prove empirically. Honestly, what need would we have to exercise faith about any of the elements of the Bible if we could prove them all to be historically true?

Then perhaps we could say that the Bible is important because it preserves timeless truths. But how is this different from other ancient texts? Why do Christians employ it instead of the texts of other ancient wisdom traditions? Why do we regard the Gospel of John as authoritative (although many of the early church fathers seemed to be suspicious of it), but not the *Gospel of Thomas*? And why is the Bible holy while Homer is not? The *Iliad* is an ancient text, and certainly it has been preserving timeless truths for people for much longer than the Bible has existed in its current form.

No, these reasons won't do either.

Why should we take the Bible seriously?

Here I bring in two scholars who have come to this question from different sides of the cultural divide, the aforementioned Marcus Borg and N. T. Wright. Both agree that the Bible presents us with a story that seems to be, in some sense, inspired by God, a story that God has created all that is; has sought us, God's creations; and has tried to bring us into the joy and light of communion. In this story, we are taught what matters: praising God, being faithful pilgrims in a community in which we experience God, caring for and loving creation itself, and expressing justice and righteousness in compassion, equity, and generosity. This story holds together, even if individual verses of the Bible seem to bounce off each other. The consistency we have been seeking is there on a macrolevel, even if we struggle on the microlevel.

Another reason that we should take the Bible seriously is because Jesus took the Bible seriously. This has been a potent argument for me, since my own formative experience of the Bible was in many ways negative: once you have had the Bible used against you as either a club or a lasso, you are inclined to regard it with some suspicion. But if you can accept on faith that Jesus was something special—which I was willing to admit, even in the days when I couldn't manage to call myself a Christian—and you can see that he knew and studied and lived out the Scriptures that were part of the Jewish tradition, then you can understand that for Jesus, the Scriptures were central to understanding God and his own life's mission.

Jesus' Scriptures would have been what we call the Hebrew Testament, by the way; the Christian Testament was not gathered in its present form until hundreds of years after Jesus died, and none of the works in it were written during Jesus' lifetime. But Jesus could retell stories from his Bible from memory in response to those who tested him, knew ancient prophecies that spoke to current situations, and in the Gospel of Luke, as we mentioned, he actually inaugurates his mission by reading from the book of Isaiah in a religious gathering:

> When he came to Nazareth, where he had been brought up, he went to the synagogue on the sabbath day, as was his custom. He stood up to read, and the scroll of the prophet Isaiah was given to him. He unrolled the scroll and found the place where it was written:
>
> > "The Spirit of the Lord is upon me,
> >   because he has anointed me to bring good news to the poor.
> > He has sent me to proclaim release to the captives
> >   and recovery of sight to the blind,
> >   to let the oppressed go free,
> >   to proclaim the year of the Lord's favor."
>
> And he rolled up the scroll, gave it back to the attendant, and sat down. The eyes of all in the synagogue were fixed on him. Then he began to say to them, "Today this scripture has been fulfilled in your hearing." (Luke 4:16–21)

If, like Bono, I accept Jesus as the walking, talking version of what God desires of us, then it seems clear that I have to take the Scriptures seriously. He did: he said here and elsewhere that he had come to fulfill them. The Scriptures led Jesus into God's will for him—along a much more challenging path than I will ever have to follow—in the same way that they can lead me.

So I would agree with Wright and Borg that we should take the Bible seriously, even if we don't necessarily read it literally. The three of us might differ a bit on how to read the Bible: Borg might say we should read it for overarching meaning, but that we shouldn't believe that its supernatural interventions are anything other than metaphorical. Wright might agree that we should read it for meaning, but argue that we should take the supernatural elements of the stories seriously as God's kingdom's inbreaking into reality. I would tell you that I have no idea if the miracles are historical fact—maybe they are, maybe they're metaphorical—but that, in a sense, it doesn't matter. As I said earlier, I believe the redemption story as a whole is true, and I've chosen to shape my life around it.

This nonliteral approach upon which we all agree suggests that you should read the Bible for story and meaning, not in tiny chunks that reinforce what you already believe (this practice, used by many Christians, is called "proof-texting," and it's what Pastor Hagee was doing with a vengeance as he wove together his tale of how his reading of the Scriptures, picking a verse from Daniel here and Revelation there, proved the republic's demise if Obama were elected). By reading for meaning, we acknowledge that the Bible that God has given us is not a systematic rule book, but a book made up mostly of narratives—and that this gathering of texts itself constitutes an overarching narrative of God's love and desire for us. We also acknowledge that it is a book (or a gathering of books) that requires interpretation, that asks for our careful thought and not just our ready acceptance of the thought of those who have gone before us.

When I teach students how to read any text, whether it's the Bible, *The Great Gatsby*, or *Battlestar Galactica*, I tell them that interpretation is an act requiring us to answer three questions: What does it say? What does it mean? And what difference does it make in our daily lives?

That is why theology matters; theology is how we personally engage those stories—and how we engage and balance the other elements we say have authority in the faith community: tradition, reason, and individual revelation. All Christians are theologians, although not necessarily conscious theologians, since all Christians acknowledge certain truths, practices, and forms of worship as their own. Still, too many Christians have left theology in the hands of "professional Christians," trusting their pastors, Sunday school teachers, bishops, and other leaders to think for them—or assuming that theology was something that could (or should) only be done by people with formal theological education or years spent immersed in the Bible.

In truth, though, theology is simply talking about God (and really—that is the literal meaning of the Greek *theo* and *logos/logy*: God talk). Andy Doyle, the Episcopal bishop of Texas, reminded me of this over coffee one morning in Austin as he argued that it is a task we all ought to be performing. Bishop Doyle remembered, "I had a professor once who told us we would all have to ask these questions. This is who I am—I have to dive into the language of my faith."

How can we know who we truly are—and who we are in relation to our Creator—if we don't talk about God, ask the hard questions, argue with long-held beliefs, and seek answers we can faithfully make our own?

Some Christians will tell you that simple faith is all that's necessary: God said it, I believe it, that settles it.

But what, exactly, did God say? We've already seen how hard it is to argue that there is one simple accessible revelation of God. If we all agreed on all of these details, would there be four major divisions of Christians in the world (Catholic, Orthodox, Anglican, and other Protestant)? Would there be twenty thousand different denominations of Christians in America alone?

I'm suggesting two things: First, we are called to encounter the Bible for ourselves, to make its story our own, to take it as seriously as Jesus did. That means reading the Bible, talking about it, learning about it, and thinking about it.

Which means, second, that we are called to do theology ourselves. We are called to examine the whys and wherefores of our faith, to discover explanations as to how a perfect and loving God can create a world that contains pain and death, to learn how our worship of God might reflect our beliefs about God, and to understand how and why the work we are called to enact on our Christian journey seems to fit into the divine story we have entered.

Doing that work faithfully will mean engaging our traditions. For Methodists, that means reading John Wesley; for Lutherans, Martin Luther; for Presbyterians, John Calvin and John Knox; and so on. For those outside a denominational framework, it should mean an earnest engagement with all these great thinkers of the church (which, honestly, would be good for all of us). It means considering the work of the thinkers who have been formative to our faith (especially those I like to call The Three A's: Augustine, Anselm, Aquinas). It means discovering theologians who have spoken to the tradition in new ways or from different perspectives, such as Martin Luther King Jr., Gustavo Gutiérrez, or Rosemary Radford Ruether. It means trying your hand at entering the contemporary theological conversation by reading such Christian thinkers as Desmond Tutu,

Rowan Williams, Kathryn Tanner, Elisabeth Schüssler Fiorenza, or John Milbank.

You may find some of these folks a challenge to understand; I do. And you may not agree with all of them; in fact, it would be schizophrenic of you to try. But if we say that authority also comes from teaching, from reason, and from our own individual response to what we read and hear and see, then we are called to active engagement with the Bible and with those who have thought, argued, and written about God.

God talk.

Since the model we are appropriating for our Christian pilgrimage is the journey, we understand that it's not enough to stand passively in one place and expect insight and experience to come to us. We have to go and seek it out for ourselves.

Finally, it's important to note that we do theology in lots of ways—and in diverse circumstances. We are doing theology when we preach or react to preaching, when we speak out for peace and justice and the environment, when we feed the hungry, when we visit the sick, when we pray, and when we worship. In all of these things, whether we realize it or not, whether we have personally worked out the theology or not, we are reaching decisions on who God is and how we are supposed to respond to God.

That leads us to one last—and in some Christian traditions, central—way we experience and understand God: through the sacraments and a sacramental understanding of the creation God has made.

And yes, this will be doing theology too.

For Further Discussion

1. What has been your experience with reading the Bible? What feelings do you have when you think about the Bible?
2. Do you think the Bible should be taken seriously—and if so, why? How should Christians in the twenty-first century approach the Bible?
3. Do you believe the Bible is a historical document? Or is it a series of stories not intended to be read historically?
4. Do you find any challenges in trying to reconcile your faith with the events chronicled in the Bible? If so, what are they?

5. What does it mean to do theology? Do you have favorite theologians (published or unpublished) who shape the way you understand your relationship with God?

For Further Reflection and Study

Marcus J. Borg, *Reading the Bible Again for the First Time: Taking the Bible Seriously but Not Literally* (San Francisco: HarperSanFrancisco, 2001). A manifesto on how we might read the Bible—and why we should. Professor Borg's work sets out a new approach to the Christian Testament that may not appeal to all, but will speak particularly to those who feel old ways of reading the Bible have made it irrelevant to twenty-first-century belief.

Peter Gomes, *The Good Book: Reading the Bible with Mind and Heart* (New York: William Morrow, 1996). The African American pastor of Harvard University outlines common ways people of all sorts misread the Bible and suggests ways for people alive and worshiping in the twenty-first century to make it their own.

Cynthia Briggs Kittredge, *Conversations with Scripture: The Gospel of John* (Harrisburg, PA: Morehouse Pub., 2007). If you've ever wondered how a thoughtful and intellectual contemporary Christian might approach a single book of the Bible, you will find a model in Professor Kittredge's book. John is a notoriously challenging Gospel, but you will understand it better—and be better prepared to reflect on it yourself—after reading this.

James L. Kugel, *How to Read the Bible: A Guide to Scripture, Then and Now* (New York: Free Press, 2007). A Bible scholar from Harvard—and a believing Jew—writes on how to reconcile the findings of biblical historical scholarship with confessional faith. A wonderful guide to the Hebrew Bible and the different ways people read it.

Brian D. McLaren, *The Secret Message of Jesus* (Nashville: Thomas Nelson, 2006). An exemplary contemporary reading of the Gospels that rescues Jesus' central message of the kingdom of God and invites us to live it in a new and relevant way. McLaren is one of the primary voices in contemporary conversations on the Bible, theology, and Christian practice.

Chapter 5

Sacramental Faith

Major Ideas

1. What sacraments are.
2. What sacraments teach us about God.
3. How sacramental faith changes us.

*T*he night before he died, Jesus was at supper with his friends. Because Jesus and those who had followed him to Jerusalem were all Jews, and because it was the Jewish Passover (the festival at which Jews celebrate the liberation of Israel from slavery in Egypt), we know that the meal had a ritual importance from the outset. But what Jesus did that night took the Jewish ritual and gave it a radical new meaning.

In the Passover story, Jews remembered how the people of Israel in Egypt had sacrificed a lamb so that they could paint their doorway with the lamb's blood—the sign for the vengeance of God to pass over their house, so that they would be saved. But in Jesus' Passover meal that night, he blessed the bread, as a good Jew should, then offered it to his friends, saying, "Take this and eat it. It is my body, which is broken for you. And whenever you eat this bread, do it to remember me."

Likewise, he took the cup of wine, prayed blessings over it, and passed it to them, saying, "Drink this, all of you. It is my blood, shed for you and for many. Whenever you drink from this cup, do it to remember me."

The radical nature of what happened at the table that night is obvious, even if the theology is complex: instead of the lamb in the Passover story, now Jesus was the one sacrificed so that those who believed in him would be saved. Somehow, in offering his body and blood, Jesus shifted the nature of God's redeeming work in the world.

Jesus did more than just command his followers to eat and drink the ritual meal that night; he was asking them to continue doing it, and to remember what he had done every time they broke bread together and passed the cup of wine (1 Corinthians 11:24–25).

This ritual meal became the central element of worship and practice in what would eventually become the Christian church; it has been repeated more times than I can imagine in the two thousand years since—think of all the churches across the world and through the centuries celebrating the Eucharist. (This fancy name for communion or the Lord's Supper, as it is also called, comes from the idea that we are celebrating a great gift from God: *eucharistia* is Greek for "thanksgiving," and we sometimes refer to the Eucharist as "The Great Thanksgiving.") But this remembrance was regarded by the early church—and still is today by those in the Catholic, Anglican, Orthodox, and other liturgical traditions—as something more than just a ceremonial reenactment of the Last Supper.

The Eucharist is a holy meal, a sacrament, in which God's power, blessing, and grace are communicated to us through the physical medium of the bread and wine. The word "sacrament" is understood by various traditions in slightly different ways. For many evangelical Christians, the sacraments have symbolic authority, but not transformative power. In other traditions, though, the sacraments are both powerful and spiritually efficacious, outward and visible signs of inward and spiritual divine grace, which means they are visible (and sometimes tangible) signs of the invisible power of God moving in the world—and in us.

One of my favorite hikes is a long climb in New Mexico's Sangre de Cristo ("blood of Christ"—how perfect is that?) Mountains, along a river up to its source, a mountain lake in a high mountaintop crater. Along the trail I often hear the wind whooshing through the treetops above, pushing around the tops of the tall spruces, even though I can't see the wind. From where I stand, I can't even feel it. But I know it's there because I see physical evidence of its invisible force, outward and visible signs of its power. (In my first hike on this trail, many years ago, a huge section of the trail was covered with towering trees that had been blown down over the winter: indisputable evidence that invisible things can have great power!) That's what the sacraments represent—the idea that the invisible power of God can move in the world with power enough to change things, including us.

Many Christians, even in emerging and evangelical Christian communities, are turning (or returning) to the Eucharist as the centerpiece of their worship together. Taking the Eucharist seriously—as something not just symbolically but also spiritually important—means that when we take communion, we are, in some very real sense, taking Christ into our bodies. We are being formed into people more like the Christ whose actions we remember when we break the bread and drink the wine. Ambrose, a fourth-century bishop from Milan, wrote that we encounter God directly through the sacraments: "You have revealed yourself to me, O Christ, face-to-face. I have met you in your sacraments." Frank Griswold, former presiding bishop of the Episcopal Church, says that the sacraments are "the Gospel enacted in ritual patterns," so for those who take the sacraments seriously, we can say that they represent another way in which God is revealed to us.[1]

When Jesus commanded his followers to reenact that Last Supper to remember him, sacramental Christians believe that he was giving us an effective way to "re-member" him again and again—to bring back together what he taught and who he was. When we take communion, we are acknowledging our desire to be more like Jesus, and we believe that God is moving through those actions that have been powerful within the tradition for many centuries. At my church in Austin, St. David's Episcopal, our rector David Boyd invites us to the table with the phrase, "May we become what we receive." It's a little like that phrase we learn when we're kids: You are what you eat.

What we are talking about here is something called sacramental theology—the idea that the Divine is mediated to us and for us by and through the physical. Just as God came to be incarnate in a human being, Jesus, so we could understand him completely, so too God's presence is offered to us in the bread and wine. (I'm not saying God is *in* the physical, which is a common mistake. God is not a coconut crème pie, although I suppose an awfully good piece of pie might be a glimpse into the holy realm, a taste of the heavenly pie, so to speak.)

The Eucharist is one of the two most important of the sacraments: the other is baptism, a ritual by which people are brought into the family of God. In some traditions, people may only be baptized when they themselves are capable of choosing it; I was brought up in such a tradition. In others, infants and children are baptized in a ritual committing the whole community of believers to walk alongside the baptized in their journey of faith until they can choose faith for themselves. In the Book of Common Prayer, a pivotal part of the service of baptism is the reaffirmation of what is called the baptismal covenant, which is done not just by the candidate for baptism and the sponsors or godparents, but by the entire fellowship of believers. In this reaffirmation, baptism becomes a communal sacrament like the Eucharist, in which everyone partakes; a new life begins in Christ, and a number of witnesses promise not only to work alongside the newly baptized, but also to reaffirm their own commitment to Christ.

Baptism and the Eucharist are also the sacraments modeled after actions of Jesus: in addition to asking his followers to celebrate the Eucharist, Jesus chose to be baptized by John the Prophet. What that might have meant for him was, we assume, different than it was for the solely human followers of John who chose to be baptized, although it remains a potent symbol for us to imitate. Chrysostom, a fourth-century Syrian bishop, noted that although John's baptism was intended for repentance, Jesus clearly had no need to repent of his sins.[2] But we do, although we also need more than simple repentance. As we've observed, the Greek word *metanoia* used in Matthew 3:8, 11 suggests not just simple repentance for sins, as the Greek is often translated, but more fully, *transformation* and *turning*. As we discover in the Gospels, the baptism of Jesus does suggest a rite of passage: some suspect that when the Spirit of the Lord descends on him as he steps from the water, there is a transformation of some sort. This is how baptism—and all the sacraments—are understood in the more-sacramental Christian traditions: the holy sacraments of the church always represent a passage or transformation for those who enter into them.

The Eucharist and baptism are both sacraments recognized by almost all Christian traditions. The Catholic, Anglican, and Orthodox traditions add others: confirmation, confession, anointing of the sick, ordination, matrimony. Each of these practices is drawn from ancient ways of relating to God; in many cases the liturgy (that is, the shape of the ritual) emerges from ancient Jewish or early Christian practices. And each seems to mark a moment in our life when we seek the presence of God—and of the Christian community—to define our passage. The sacraments may represent significant moments on our journey, often transformations from one stage of life to another. For example, confirmation demonstrates the mature affirmation of a relationship with Christ after baptism. Marriage, the anointing of the sick and dying, ordination to ministry or priesthood, and confession—rituals in which one acknowledges failings, asks forgiveness, and turns (there's that *metanoia* again) away from sin and toward a reformed life—all of these represent moments when we are moving from one thing to the next. Since these changes are marked by Christian ritual, we are connected to Christ, as well as to the Christian community, the believers who provide strength, comfort, and wisdom as individuals move from one state to another.

This sacramental worldview is in direct opposition to the worldview of many contemporary Christians, who are, in the words of Brian McLaren, choosing evacuation and abdication: "If the earth is a lost cause to you, then you will abandon this life and world for the afterlife. You will choose the way of withdrawal, isolation, self-protection, and self-distancing."[3] This is a potent but accurate understanding of the Christianity I was first taught, one that assumed that this world was, at best, unnecessary, and at worst, an evil distraction from the only thing that mattered: heaven.

A sacramental understanding of life and faith redirects us to the world around us. Rather than rejecting the physical world because it is not the spiritual world—a form of early Christian heresy called Gnosticism—it embraces the possibility of experiencing God as the divine is mediated through the physical. Those who follow the way of Christ serve a God who created this world of matter, who was willing to enter into this world as a human being so that we could know God, and who committed the Holy Spirit to comfort, challenge, and inspire us here today.

This shift in worldview will make a great difference both in how we view the world and in how we live our lives. First, it should shift us away from the old Christian worldview that we are the masters of creation and thus can use it—or use it up—as we wish. As Rowan

Williams writes, a sacramental understanding of reality insists that "a degree of reverence and humility is appropriate when we approach anything in the created order." Williams explains that this understanding will cure us from the mind-set that has led us to ecological crisis, our former inability to think of the world as related to God's mystery, rather than simply a "huge warehouse of stuff to be used for our convenience."[4] If the physical world can be a vehicle for transcendence, or for connection to the Divine, then it must be treated with more respect; within sacramental faith lies a new theology of conservation and a new love for creation.

Sacramental faith also suggests the possibility that all of creation may offer us windows into the mind of God—not just as a mountain lake, shimmering like diamonds under a cloudless blue sky, but also less-exalted creations. The movie *American Beauty*, written by the Christian writer and producer Alan Ball, presents a convincing argument that we catch a glimpse of the sacred in even something as mundane—or seemingly profane—as a discarded plastic bag, dancing in the wind. Ball's film also suggests that we may receive a revelation of the Divine from human creations. After all, human beings are a part of this creation, which offers us a glimpse of the holy.

With discernment, we can say that God is constantly speaking to those with ears to hear, and that in human art, architecture, music, and storytelling, we may also hear God's voice when the art itself is true and beautiful.

A few months ago I stood in front of a painting by the Spanish painter El Greco, *The Penitent St. Peter*. It was lit so that the figure of the saint seemed to glow, and it was very much like being in church; I had the same feeling that I have when I receive—or serve—communion. Not that the picture itself was possessed of power, mind you—I don't think *The Penitent St. Peter* is holy, in the sense that it radiates inherent sacred value. But as I looked at the painting—and as I gave myself to the possibility that the Creator of the universe might have something to communicate to me in this created work—I felt that I was receiving at least some piece of what God had for me. As Diana Butler Bass puts it, "Art reaches toward God, where humanity touches divinity, and where the intellectual fades to apprehending beauty."[5] In this moment of beauty, I felt the touch of God.

I would argue (and have, in other books) that God can speak to us in more than just "great art," the classics, and the traditional, although certainly I have felt God's presence in Handel and stained glass and the Canterbury Cathedral. But as the *American Beauty* example suggests, popular culture has been an important part of my spiritual journey as well, as it has been for many people, particularly younger generations. As Bishop Doyle notes, we can learn from younger believers how to be open to God's presence in many things—although he adds a necessary caution: "Young people seek meaning in ways that older people don't, and that's a benefit to us. They see meaning in lots of different things—they have an eye to faith that is broader. But seeing meaning in everything must be tempered by the fact that what they think is important may not be."

It was young people who caught on to the spiritual value of *The Matrix*, sensing that amid the kung fu and computer-generated imagery, a serious conversation was taking place around commitment, salvation, and the Chosen One or Messiah. For many years, young people have understood that members of U2 were not only trying to live a life of faith, but also communicating important elements of that faith through their music. And more recently, young people who have grown up on Harry Potter have begun living lives in some way shaped by those books and movies—lives that reflect the clear Christian messages of calling, community, sacrifice, and redemption to be found in J. K. Rowling's story.

I think, in fact, of Adam Clayton, U2's bassist and "non-Christian" member, saying that when they got started, U2's music didn't sound like something you would hear on the radio: it sounded, instead, like something you should hear in church. Even those who are not followers of Jesus can feel when God is breaking into this world through words, music, and images.

So the challenge—one that has been taken up by faith communities offering "popcorn theology" evenings or discussing my book *The Gospel according to Hollywood* in Sunday school classes—is to responsibly add an additional source of revelation to those we've included so far: creation. God may be—and experience suggests, is—speaking to us through the novels of Leif Enger and Marilynne Robinson and Lee Smith, through the essays of Anne Lamott and Dennis Covington and Annie Dillard, through the music of Patti Griffin and

Bruce Springsteen and the Reverend Al Green. Our job is to listen—and to ask ourselves, what does God have to say to me in this?

It's also important for us to understand that God may be using works that don't seem immediately obvious; over the years I have written and spoken on how the violent and profane film *Pulp Fiction* taught me vital lessons about grace and God's movement in the world, although many people couldn't get past the bullets—and F-bombs—to hear God speaking. Two more-recent films that I often discuss as filled with theological import are also filled with unremitting evil: *No Country for Old Men* and *The Dark Knight*. And yet, these beautifully made and challenging films present a true vision of a world where good does not always conquer evil.

To be a true follower of Jesus is to wrestle with the implications of that, with God's place in suffering and death. It's also to recognize that in life—as in these films—moments of grace and human goodness can pierce what seems to be unremitting darkness. Rowan Williams, who is a poet and a lover of popular culture as well as a theologian and archbishop, has on a number of occasions written that Christian art must portray the entire range of creation, since God—in the person of Christ—was willing to die for all of creation, not just the pretty parts, not just the beautiful people. As Williams puts it, "There are no areas that are essentially off-limits if God is truly the Creator of *this* world."[6]

Sacramental faith, then, takes in the whole idea that God's grace can be conveyed to us by physical reality: by the sacred ceremonies of the church—the Eucharist, the water of baptism, the oil for anointing the sick and dying—by the beauty and terror of the created world, and by the power and inspiration of art. These experiences along the way emphasize the idea that we are growing, maturing in the faith, traveling on the Way, and not frozen in place following a pivotal faith decision. In sacramental theology, salvation is not a moment, but a process, a becoming rather than a being. God is still—ever—shaping us.

And because we are people in process, we don't rest on our laurels, secure in our salvation. We seek out the sacraments, which draw us toward God. We seek ways to experience additional closeness with God.

And that leads us to spiritual practice—the habits and work of followers of Jesus who want to draw ever nearer to the God of creation.

For Further Discussion

1. How do you understand sacraments like communion and baptism? Has that understanding changed over the years? Why?
2. What does it mean to you to notice that the two central sacraments of Christian faith are modeled on sacramental moments in Jesus' life?
3. Have you ever felt a sense of holy connection to God through the created world? When and where were you? What did you remember of the experience after it was over?
4. Has a work of art or popular culture ever given you a spiritual insight? Have you ever felt yourself comforted in despair by a song or story?

For Further Study and Reflection

Greg Garrett, *The Gospel according to Hollywood* (Louisville, KY: Westminster John Knox Press, 2007). The "Gospel according to" series is the best-known of the recent studies of religion and popular culture. My book on how Hollywood films can transmit sacred truths and open up theological questions shows sacramental faith at work.

Flannery O'Connor, *Mystery and Manners: Occasional Prose* (New York: Farrar, Straus & Giroux, 1969). One of the greatest Christian artists of the past hundred years reflects on her own fiction and on the making of Christian art.

Alexander Schmemann, *For the Life of the World: Sacraments and Orthodoxy* (Crestwood, NY: St. Vladimir's Press, 1997). A Greek Orthodox sacramental theology that convincingly argues for not only the sacred nature of the formal sacraments but also a sacramental way of life.

Rowan Williams, *Grace and Necessity: Reflections on Art and Love* (London: Continuum, 2005). Williams, himself a renowned poet and literary critic, argues for the validity of art and beauty—broadly defined—to mediate God's presence to us. A challenging but worthwhile little book.

Chapter 6

Spiritual Practice

Major Ideas
1. What spiritual practice is.
2. Why spiritual practice matters.
3. Christian wisdom traditions that could have value for your journey.

*I*n his memoir, *A Pilgrimage of Faith*, the legendary Baptist seminary professor Henlee Barnette told a story that illustrates the different spiritual understandings we have been discussing in this book. "Christianity," he wrote, "is a way of life undergirded by faith in God. I once said this in a sermon. A deacon [leader] of the church approached me and informed me that he had been a deacon in that church for twenty years and never thought of Christianity as a way of life."[1] In that respect, unfortunately, this deacon probably represents many of the ordinary Christians in the pews.

For far too many Christians, Christianity is largely affirming a belief in God, and it is lived out through church attendance and adherence to some standard of personal piety. It's not, as surveys have told us, necessarily spiritual, and many who attend church may not even have an authentic experience of God.

Like Barnette, we have described Christian faith in this book as a way of life, a journey rather than an arrival; as Ms. Angelou told me, Christianity is not something we have accomplished, but something we do. If we think of faith as active, then the idea of practice provides some important insights for us. My son Jake is a personal trainer who works out almost every day. He does not rest on his laurels, assuming that he has achieved fitness and is as healthy as he will ever be. Instead, like anyone who wants to do something well and who has made that thing a priority, he sets aside time every day for further work, refinement, and practice. So we too are called to work toward a greater humanity, a greater faith, and a greater participation in creation as part of our redemption, and traditionally, spiritual practice has been one of the primary ways that happens.

But what does practice mean in our buy-it-now culture, particularly when Christianity has been branded as a onetime decision rather than a way of life? How can we cultivate the spirit of faith-in-progress we will need to undertake the long journey?

Here is where the history of Christian tradition—the record of those saints who have gone before us and left powerful examples of Christian expression and spirituality—can be invaluable to us. Saint Isaac of Syria wrote some seventeen hundred years ago that the task of our lives is to cultivate a compassionate heart. A compassionate heart is the goal of our spiritual practice and will be the well from which we give cool water to ourselves and the other thirsty souls we encounter on our journey. But as the former presiding bishop of the Episcopal Church Frank Griswold points out, the first step on our journey comes when we ask the difficult question, "Do I want to have a compassionate heart?" Unless we can answer that question in the affirmative, then we will not enter into the hard work involved, because to have a compassionate heart calls us to a lifetime of spiritual homework.[2]

But if the answer is affirmative, then our tradition gives us tools and inspiring examples that can lead us on paths that will enlarge and engage our souls. Spirituality is the fuel for our Christian journeys, and four major Christian traditions—the Desert, Celtic, Benedictine, and Franciscan—can help us to cultivate compassionate hearts and to grow in faith and love of God.

The Wisdom of the Desert

We'll turn first to wisdom from the Desert tradition. In the third century, Christians fled from cities into the deserts of Sinai, Egypt, and

Syria, discovering a more authentic Christianity by seeking their most genuine selves. The message of the desert is one we understand today: strip away all that is false and unnecessary about yourself, and what is left is the true you. These Desert fathers and mothers lived in an era in which their countercultural faith had suddenly become the official religion of the world's greatest empire. In a world where faith was beginning to seem tainted by culture, withdrawal seemed like a good idea, and so these fathers and mothers moved far enough away from civilization so that they could live simply and authentically—although not so far away from each other that they could not gather for worship, support, and accountability.

One of the fathers—Abbot Moses of Scete—left us this bit of wisdom: "Go, sit in your cell, and your cell will teach you everything." This is truly countercultural wisdom. It's harder than ever today to sit in one's cell without white noise of one kind or another. And yet, how can we truly know ourselves unless we turn off the TV and computer, unplug the iPod, and stop moving at light speed for a moment? Contemporary life is the enemy of personal reflection—and without reflection, without attention to ourselves and our souls, we cannot have an authentic relationship with God. The Desert mothers and fathers understood that reflection—a willingness to disengage from our daily lives, if only for a bit, and take stock of ourselves, our relationships with others, and our relationship with God—is at the heart of spiritual practice. Jesus knew this. In the Gospels, we often see him withdrawing from the crowds, going up on a mountain to pray, and his behavior seems psychologically and spiritually acute. He knew what he needed in order to do the work to which he was called.

Every year or two at Baylor, I teach Henry David Thoreau's *Walden*, a nineteenth-century American version of the desert journey of reflection. Thoreau built a tiny cabin on the shore of Walden Pond, a mile away from the nearby town of Concord, and spent two years there observing the world and himself in minute detail. Thoreau was not a Christian, as we understand classic confession, but he was a person of great insight and spiritual wisdom. He lived in an America that was just becoming urbanized and learning to communicate at great speed, and he recognized that if he wasn't careful, this life full of information could, paradoxically, leave him bereft of meaning.

"I went to the woods because I wished to live deliberately," Thoreau said, to discover what was truly important in life, "and not, when I came to die, discover that I had not lived."[3] Life will not slow down or stop for you, except in moments of great tragedy or loss, and at those times, you probably will not feel like doing the hard work of reflection. So if you don't consciously take time to reflect, life will hustle you on to the end of the line, and upon arriving there, you may discover that you have not lived—or at least, have not lived a life that truly matters.

When we study Thoreau, one or more of my students always tells me, "I can't go away from the world. I've got responsibilities—school, work, friends, family. How am I supposed to withdraw and examine myself?"

It's certainly harder for those of us who remain caught up in the culture than for those who went off to the desert—or the pond. But there are still some practical things from the Desert tradition that we can adopt. First: simplicity. What can you eliminate from your life, what things can you do without, what noise can you silence so that you can begin to see yourself without so much interference? Every year I lead a weeklong retreat in the New Mexico desert, where we are (except for the occasional offensive BlackBerry) cut off from the outside world for days on end.

We slow down.

We listen.

We spend part of the time in silence, part in prayer, and part in meditation, asking ourselves hard questions about who we are and what we truly want.

And more often than not, we begin to receive some answers.

Perhaps you can't get away from your life for an entire week. But can you remove yourself for a morning? Can you turn off your iPod, your cell phone, your TV? Can you, even for a little while, step away from Facebook and texting and our whole spiritually-disastrous wired existence, which may interrupt you dozens—or hundreds—of times a day? Can you simply sit or lie down or walk and pay attention to yourself instead of letting yourself be dragged this way and that by all the demands that your life places upon you?

If you can do that, you can begin to perform the act of self-examination that the Desert tradition demands. And when you can be honest with yourself about where you are, what you need, and what improvements must occur, you can begin to take steps to implement those changes.

The Desert tradition teaches other things besides the value of silence and simplicity. It teaches us, for example, to be honest concerning our faults and failures—and generous with those of our neighbors. It teaches us that while we need our own space for reflection, we are saved alongside our brothers and sisters. We'll see some of these things again in later Christian traditions, but the Desert fathers and mothers are, in many ways, at the heart of Christian spirituality.

The Celtic Tradition

At first it might seem disorienting to go from the deserts of the Middle East to the green lands of Scotland, Ireland, and England, but the Celtic tradition has a clear line of descent from the Desert tradition. You have only to take a look at some of the stone huts built on the edge of the wild North Sea to realize that those Irish and Scottish monks and hermits were simply living in a different sort of desert, employing another kind of isolation in search of their authentic selves and the faith that would make life meaningful. But the Celtic tradition differs in some important ways: unlike other forms of Christianity that sought God primarily within the walls of a church, the Celtic tradition looked outside, into the wildness of sea and sky and hill and forest, and found God present there. The early Celtic Christians gathered for worship beside mammoth carved-stone outdoor crosses, not inside elaborate stone churches. That orientation toward finding God in the world around us represents one of the most important spiritual legacies of the Celtic tradition.

Rather than imagining God as distant and lofty, the Celts saw God—and indeed, all three persons of the Trinity—as immanent and available. Celtic prayers acknowledge the near presence of God, saints, and angels, and these prayers were said over even the most mundane tasks—turning the cows out into the pasture, starting the morning fire, weaving on a loom. That awareness of God's presence in all things suggests, again, a practice of mindfulness: how might God be speaking to you in the silence, in the sunlight, in the words and music of your favorite song? Cultivating a sense of God's presence can also help you to have a sense of strength and comfort for the heavy lifting that comes on the journey.

In 664 a synod (a fancy word for a big church meeting) was held in Whitby in northern England between representatives of Celtic and Roman Christianity. It was a confrontation between two different understandings of Christianity, characterized by representative saints: John (known in Celtic tradition as the beloved disciple who reclined on Christ's breast at the Last Supper, listening to the heartbeat of God) and Peter (known in Roman tradition as the disciple on whom Jesus said he would build the church). It was a collision of two understandings: the Celtic understanding of God's presence at the heart of all life, and the emphasis on goodness of creation and revelation through creation—as opposed to the Roman mission of holiness within tradition and the walls of the church.

At the Synod of Whitby, as you can guess from history, the Roman mission was declared the dominant one. This was tragic for Christians not because we don't experience God through our church traditions and within formal worship, but because the Celtic way was lost, almost irretrievably, before its gradual reclamation within the last two hundred years. In its return, we rediscover the idea of God's loving presence in a world that some Christian traditions have assigned to Satan. We are reminded of the lesson we began to learn from the Desert mothers and fathers: pay attention. Not just to yourself and your prayers (as the Desert teaches), but also to the world, because God may be found all around.

The Celtic understanding of holy presence goes so far as to say that Jesus walks alongside us. One of my favorite Celtic prayers says simply,

> The path I walk,
> Christ walks it.

When we imagine Jesus as companion on the journey (a frequent topic of Celtic prayer and liturgy) or think of ourselves as surrounded by the great company of the saints, we know that even when we are lonely, we are not alone. When we imagine that God is always working in the world around us, that God can be present to us in wind and wave and mountain as well as in church and in praise songs, we open up an emphasis that has not been a focus of mainstream Christianity for centuries. And though we don't want to go too far in the direction of immanence—God is revealed *through* nature, but God is not a rock or a tree or a mountain—this is a valuable corrective to the church's decision at Whitby to focus on the Roman vision of faith and practice.

The Benedictine Rule

So: reflection. Awareness. But how can we pattern our lives in such a way that these things become possible? The Benedictine tradition opens a way for us here. Almost fifteen hundred years ago, Benedict gathered a group of Christians in community, and knowing how difficult it is for us to live together even when we congregate under the banner of God's love for us, Benedict wrote down a set of practical and spiritual guidelines for Christian community: the Benedictine Rule.

Bishop Greg Rickel has found great strength and wisdom within the Benedictine tradition:

> I have a Rule of Life following the Benedictine model of Stability, Obedience, and Conversion of Life, with Hospitality laden throughout. I like the Benedictine take on the Christian walk, that of doing ordinary things extraordinarily well. In other words, prayer is the act of all we do, not something to be sequestered in a church or closet.

We find several nuggets of wisdom in Bishop Rickel's statement. First, he reminds us of the Rule of St. Benedict, the ancient document that prescribes how monks and nuns should live holy lives of prayer and work in community, and it still has much to teach us today. The Rule has been read and followed for fifteen hundred years by men and women around the world, in sacred communities and outside the walls of churches, convents, and monasteries. Like Bishop Rickel, we can also develop a Rule of Life for ourselves to follow daily, making certain that those things that feed our souls and bring us closer to God are a part of our daily, weekly, or monthly practice. How often would you like to pray? To read the Bible? To worship? To get away from technology for reflection? To spend time rowing or hiking or cycling to encounter God in nature?

The Benedictine Rule establishes daily alternating times of prayer and work; the idea of fixed-hour prayer is a radical change for many people, who pray mostly when they must. But as Bishop Rickel suggests, the Benedictine way recognizes that there is no essential difference between work and prayer. We might pray formally at morning, noon, and evening, for example—but we could also grow to understand that we are praying when we do our best at whatever task God has set in front of us. Buddhist monk Thich Nhat Hanh often tells a story about how he grew to love washing dishes, a task he had once despised, because he came to understand that by doing it consciously instead of simply rushing through it, he could offer that mundane task up as prayer and as love for his fellow monks. It's what he, in perhaps his best-known book, calls "The Miracle of Mindfulness."

Prayer through dishwashing? Why not? There are a hundred ways to fall and kiss the ground, the Persian poet Rumi affirms, and prayer comes in many more ways than just our bowing our heads and closing our eyes. By paying attention to our lives and offering all of them up to God, we can attain some of the rhythms that the Benedictine Rule describes in prayer and work, including the recognition that in a life full of awareness, we are constantly praying.

Franciscan Compassion

The Franciscan Tradition—which grows from the life and teaching of St. Francis of Assisi—began as a monastic tradition, like the Benedictine Order, and also reflects some immediate similarities to the Celtic way of spirituality. Francis loved all God's creatures, saw them as brothers and sisters, and saw God as present in creation. These ideas could make a huge difference in how Christians see their relationship to the world in which we live. But perhaps more important for us, Francis also modeled the compassion of Christ in all he did, calling those Franciscan brothers and sisters who gathered around his example into solidarity with the poor and with all those who suffer.

Francis's example inspires us to seek out and comfort the hungry, the sick, and the needy. It offers a way to take the spiritual energy we have been storing up in contemplation, prayer, and awareness and pay it forward. In practicing the Franciscan way, we pray for and seek to serve those who are less fortunate, a part of Christian practice that has become more and more important in recent years, even in many conservative Christian traditions.

After Hurricane Katrina devastated the Gulf Coast and all but destroyed New Orleans, the response from the U.S. government was, shall we say, lackluster. But the response from people of faith was monumental and ongoing. Christians from the mainline Protestant traditions that had always believed in the importance of such work were joined by Catholics, who have a long tradition of peace-and-justice work, and by members of evangelical congregations—all intent on serving those who suffered. Together they showed the world that Christian faith in action, modeling the compassion of Christ, can make a difference in the world.

Francis became a monk, but he was also an incendiary personality who stood against many of the institutional understandings of Christianity. He renounced personal wealth, called the church into solidarity with the poor and suffering, and patched up a falling-down church building, a metaphor for what might be done for the larger church. Like Benedict, the Desert mothers and fathers, and the Celtic saints, a community formed around Francis and his beliefs. This community lived simply, worked with the poor and unfortunate, and followed a rule of life that made their spiritual journey more possible.

Francis's attempts to be Christlike are at the heart of the modern quest to discern the answer to the question "What would Jesus do?" To live like Francis is to ask that question continuously; late in his life, Francis allegedly developed stigmata, wounds that mimicked the ones Christ received in his crucifixion. For Francis, the desire to live in Christlike love, humility, and service even reshaped his body.

For us, at the very least, it could reshape our lives.

Each of these Christian traditions (and others besides) offers us the opportunity to cultivate a compassionate heart, pay more attention to our lives, and begin to be shaped more like Jesus than like the world in which we live. Through the awareness that we too are called to pray, to reflect on Scripture, to live in community, and to work for the salvation of the world, we can cut through many of the things that don't matter about Christian faith and reconnect with the things that do.

For Further Discussion

1. How do you feel about silence? Do you regularly spend time without outside stimuli, or do you feel that you must have noise or distraction most of your waking hours?
2. Do you see the created world as good or evil? Would it change your ideas about creation—or concerning God—to believe that the world is inherently good?
3. Take a look at your calendar: Do you have work events listed? Social events? Spiritual events? Could you imagine planning how and when you might pray, worship, read the Bible or spiritual literature, or go on retreat? Would you find it easier to maintain spiritual disciplines if they were planned in advance?
4. What would it look like in your own life to live the compassion of Christ as Francis did? What practical steps could you take to help the poor, feed the hungry, or minister to "the least of these"?

For Further Study and Reflection

Joan Chittister, *Wisdom Distilled from the Daily: Living the Rule of St. Benedict Today* (New York: HarperCollins, 1991). Chittister, herself a lifelong follower of the Benedictine tradition, explains how the Rule can shape our lives today.

Brian D. McLaren, *Finding Our Way Again: The Return of the Ancient Practices* (Nashville: Thomas Nelson, 2008). In this first of a series of books on recovering the devotional practices of the church, McLaren reacquaints us with contemplation, prayer, and mysticism.

J. Philip Newell, *Listening to the Heartbeat of God* (Mahwah, NJ: Paulist Press, 1997). This is a fine one-book introduction to Celtic Christianity. Newell has also composed several books of Celtic prayers; his *Celtic Benediction* has been important in my own daily spiritual practice.

Barbara Brown Taylor, *An Altar in the World: The Geography of Faith* (San Francisco: HarperOne, 2009). One of my favorite spiritual guides writes on the spiritual practices that should make up the life of mature faith—reverence, prayer, Sabbath, blessings, and others—with her characteristic honesty and beauty.

Benedicta Ward, ed., *The Desert Fathers: Sayings of the Early Christian Monks* (New York: Penguin, 2003). A strong collection of the Desert sayings organized by spiritual theme; here you can listen to the wisdom of the Desert story by story. Remember that these are dense sayings that emerge from a different culture than our own; some may speak to you and some may not.

Chapter 7

Sin and Salvation

Major Ideas

1. What constitutes sin.
2. Why we require forgiveness and salvation.
3. How we understand Jesus' life, death, and resurrection.

*O*n Sunday mornings during my youth, I remember singing a chorus from the Baptist Hymnal. An old gospel hymn suggested everything we were supposed to know about sin and redemption:

> Are you washed in the blood,
> In the soul-cleansing blood of the Lamb?
> Are your garments spotless? Are they white as snow?
> Are you washed in the blood of the Lamb?[1]

Many American Christians have accepted the truth of this formulation: When they accept Jesus as their Savior—that is, when they assent to the faith statement that Jesus is Lord—their sins, which are as scarlet (traditionally an infamous color, as in *The Scarlet Letter*) are washed away, and they, as individuals, are made pure and sinless. Whatever bad things they may have done—and their own fallenness, the result of their human nature—are swept away, forgotten. They are now creatures of God rather than creatures of the devil—or of the world.

But what is sin, precisely?

Why do we need to be saved from it?

How are we saved, if indeed we are?

It's in these questions that we find some dissension among Christians—and some difficulties for contemporary Christianity. A prominent formulation in American churches is that the world is fallen, that human beings partake of an original sin that taints all their efforts to be righteous without God's intervention, and that sin consists largely of a series of immoral acts or attitudes. The possibility of salvation—that all sin can be washed clean if you will only believe—leads directly to many of the tendencies that nonbelievers have noted as most objectionable about Christianity: empty moralism; hypocrisy; irrelevance.

A focus on morality rather than on God leads Christians to be judgmental, to single out sexual sins (especially homosexual acts) as particularly dangerous, to become involved in political debate and action in order to mandate a political version of morality consistent with their codes, and to appear hypocritical when—as sometimes happens—their speech and their behavior aren't consistent. Every time a conservative Christian shows that he (and it is almost always "he") is only human and is caught in a homosexual affair, an addiction, or in some other moral scandal, it only confirms what many people believe to be worst about Christianity: that Christians at heart are only hypocrites who act holier than thou but are just as sinful as everyone else. (Worse, really. Everyone actually is sinful, but Christians claim to be redeemed and make pronouncements on how bad everyone else is when they are exactly the same.)

Conservative Christians pay too much attention to sin, particularly if it is individual sin; partly in reaction to this tendency, progressive Christians often pay too little, unless it is societal sin. So let's start by paying enough attention to sin, and see if we can reformulate our understanding of sin so that it fits more closely with the idea of the Christian journey we've been pursuing, rather than as a set of "Thou Shalt Nots."

Defining Sin

First, what is sin?

I think all Christians could agree that there is something in the human condition or in human life that distances us from God. Paul

Tillich and other theologians have said that sin is that which separates us from God, but they go further: sin also separates us from
others, and from our own essential selves, the selves God wants us to
be. So sin is something—a choice or a behavior—that separates us
from everything that truly matters.

But the old sins—those of morality, sexuality, and so forth—not
only seem less and less relevant in a rapidly changing world; they
also don't encompass the whole range of things that separate us
from God, each other, and ourselves. I have a dear Christian friend,
for example, who is one-half of a lifetime same-sex partnership.
According to many members of my family and to most conservative American Christians, my friend may profess Christianity (in my
observation, he seems to be living one of the most faithful lives I
know), but his unwillingness to abandon the "sin" of homosexual
relations will be his damnation. At the same time, other Christians
sift the biblical and theological evidence and conclude that while a
sexual relationship that exploits another or is entered into without
mutual love and respect may indeed be sinful, there is nothing un-
Christian in a relationship in which love, respect, and mutual care
appear, whether or not that relationship is sealed by marriage.

And in some parts of the developed world, such debates over sexual morality seem archaic: I concur with those who suggest that one
hundred years from now, the religious debate over homosexuality
will look as ridiculous as the ones on those moral issues from my
youth: horse racing and liquor by the drink.

Thinking of sin purely in terms of things we should not do ignores
the fact that there is so much we are called to do—and don't. The liturgy of confession in the Book of Common Prayer begins in this way:

> Most merciful God,
> we confess that we have sinned against you
> in thought, word, and deed,
> by what we have done,
> and by what we have left undone.
> We have not loved you with our whole heart;
> we have not loved our neighbors as ourselves.
> We are truly sorry and we humbly repent.

This confession highlights some useful understandings concerning
sin: that it can be internal or external, that words can be harmful

(Buddhists speak of the necessity for right speech), and that the sins we have committed are no more important than our failure to do the things we ought to have done. When we don't love God or our neighbors wholeheartedly, we are as guilty of sin as if we'd cheated on our partner or embezzled from our employer.

But if we can't simply say that sin is a set of things we *shouldn't* do (the Ten Commandments or some such thing, with a few contemporary amendments), then what is sin?

Theologians like Augustine and Aquinas might tell us that sin is disordered desire. For example, in and of itself, sex is a beautiful gift from God, but in our selfish drive for our own pleasure and satisfaction, we have often broken human sexuality into disordered desires. Examples of this would be promiscuity, pornography, prostitution, and a variety of other sexual sins in which people are degraded (or degrade themselves), in which we treat others without the respect that God calls us to exercise, and in which our satisfaction of the moment is allowed to scar and even to destroy lives. Sexual trafficking, sexual addiction, broken relationships, sexually transmitted disease, and warped priorities all grow out of these disordered desires. (And I'm as guilty of an unhealthy focus on sex as the next man, although as the years go by I'm beginning to identify with something my late friend Frank Leavell used to say: "Lust used to be my favorite of the Deadly Sins, but Gluttony is coming up fast on the inside." We always have disordered desires, even if they change at different seasons of life.)

Our disordered desire comes from our human nature. In this, at least, I am in agreement with Augustine, who formulated the idea of original sin that has become a Christian dogma. While I don't agree with him that this sin is passed on from parent to child, and has been since humans lived in the garden of Eden (partly because I don't believe there ever was such a place), I do agree that by our very nature, we humans are prone to seek our own pleasures, and that choosing our own wills over the will of God for us distances us from God, from each other, from God's creation, and from our best selves. Sin has power over us because we are more likely—to paraphrase J. K. Rowling—to choose what is easy instead of what is right.[2] When we make those choices often enough, our lives are distorted by them, and in a real sense, we become slaves to our sin. Aristotle wrote that action was character; existentialist philosophy holds that we are defined by our choices; virtue ethics says that we are what we repeatedly do. In other words, our actions make us who we are.

So sin arises out of human selfishness, disordered desires, and inability to make right choices. It can become a habit or pervasive behavior that separates us from all that matters. My own belief is that this is a result of our fallen humanity, rather than the action of Satan, but some Christians believe that there is a cosmic tempter who leads us into evil. I have to confess that I don't see much need for one; I have been capable of plenty of evil out of my own selfish nature and brokenness. I'd be glad, in fact, for the excuse of a powerful cosmic evil, but I think you can quickly see how this could be an easy way out. The book of James in the Christian Testament tells us that "one is tempted by one's own desire, being lured and enticed by it; then, when that desire has conceived, it gives birth to sin, and that sin, when it is fully grown, gives birth to death" (James 1:14–15).

I must be responsible for the evil I have done and the good I have not done.

And I will confess that without God's help, I might hope for change, but I can't see my way to it.

Embracing Redemption

This change moves us in the direction of redemption, from darkness to light, from death toward life. Like "sin," "redemption" means different things to various faith traditions. In vast stretches of American Christianity, to say you are "saved" means that you have asked Jesus to cleanse you of your sins. Certainly the Bible suggests a decision of some sort, an awareness, a remorse. Both the Hebrew Testament and the Christian Testament call for a turning away from sin and toward a new life (as in "We are truly sorry and we humbly repent"), although in a larger sense than simple renunciation of evil actions. While one might repent of drinking to excess, sleeping with prostitutes, or beating one's children, that repentance needs to be accompanied by what is called "amendment of life." We don't just stop the bad practices, but we begin—or return to—the good.

Since this is a human decision, we are participants in our own salvation, but Christians believe that in and of ourselves we are incapable of achieving it. No amount of spiritual practice, navel-gazing, or fervent prayer will save us. That's where God comes in, and the old rugged cross, and the empty tomb.

Although again, you'll see that there's a vast difference in the way old and new Christianity might understand salvation and God's place in it.

Christianity 1.0 has a way of understanding salvation that seems to echo Scott Cairns's poem "The Spiteful Jesus" in its stories of an angry God who could probably benefit from some therapy to work through his anger issues. According to this story of salvation, God gave us over to destruction because of our sin and rebellion, but Jesus, who was God yet also human, offered himself in atonement for our sins, to pay the price that our sins demanded: death. With the action of this great high priest, sacrifice appeased the angry God and canceled the debt we owed because of our sins.

For over a thousand years the doctrine of atonement has been at the heart of Christian understanding, although pursuing the angry God may require us to tell some stories that seem to be in conflict with other stories we tell about God: If God loves us, then why would our rebellion require our destruction? If God knows all, then why would God set up our irrevocable punishment, knowing our human propensity toward sin and selfishness? And if Jesus is God's Son (as well as being God), what sort of Father demands (or accepts) the death of his own Son to pay a debt to himself?

If such questions have ever occurred to you—or bounced you out of belief—then you might be relieved to know that "substitutionary atonement," the doctrine that Jesus died to pay the cost of our sins, is not the only game in town. Believers have discovered other ways to understand Jesus' death that don't require that we tell stories of a sadistic or legalistic God. God's justice can be something other than punitive or vengeful when we begin to consider alternative meanings of the crucifixion and resurrection.

Greek Orthodox icons of the resurrection feature Jesus emerging from the tomb—and with one hand, lifting tiny figures of Adam and Eve, representing humanity, from their tombs. What if Jesus' death was not in response to a need for justice, but in response to the created world's natural movement toward sin and death? What if Jesus' death—and God's raising of Jesus from the dead—can be seen as

God's victory over those tragic elements of creation, as God's rescue of all of creation, instead of a narrow legalistic pardon of those individuals who have transgressed? Brian McLaren says that he eventually rejected legalistic individual salvation in favor of the belief that Jesus is the Savior of the entire world, and that Jesus' death and resurrection have put this plan into action. This is the idea I'd like to pursue as we conclude our brief survey of salvation.

For Rowan Williams, the death and resurrection of Jesus Christ also have a meaning other than as a punitive sacrifice to a powerful God. Resurrection is not, he says, centered on hope for the guilty so much as it is a story of God's grace for us: not "the vindication of a divine plan [but] the uncovering of all forgotten wounds, so as to open up again the possibility of fresh relation, growth into healing."[3] The healing of the universe is a frequent theme of theologians who understand the crucifixion and resurrection as cosmic events, but not necessarily as judiciary ones.

N. T. Wright has also argued against any interpretations of the resurrection event that don't include the recognition that it is the universal victory of God over the forces of evil; like the Greek Orthodox icons, Wright suggests that "when Jesus rose again, God's whole creation emerged from the tomb, introducing a world full of new potential and possibility. Indeed, precisely because part of that new possibility is for human beings themselves to be revived and renewed, the resurrection of Jesus doesn't leave us as passive, helpless spectators."[4] In other words, as Wright interprets the story of salvation, redemption isn't our being rescued from our sins so much as it is a divine reordering of the world in which we are permitted to participate.

Think about Harry Potter. (Spoiler alert: I'm going to talk about the end of the series here.) It's the seventh book, the final film. In the end of this grand saga of good, evil, and human choice, Harry Potter chooses to go to his death. It's a death that he trusts will have impact, but there's no way he can know this for sure. He believes it's part of a larger plan, but really, agreeing to die without a struggle—although it's exactly what we're told Jesus did—can't come easily for most people.

But in the story, Harry's death, offered up in love as a heroic sacrifice, not only defeats the evil powers that stood in the way of human happiness. It also inaugurates a new day of peace and understanding, and if people aren't standing around singing "Kumbaya" (if in fact they have ever done that in Britain), there's still the sense that this death and resurrection have changed the world. They have caused a new freedom, tolerance, and compassion to burst across the globe, which without Harry's sacrifice would have been darkened by selfishness, evil, and death. Harry chose to die to rescue the world and everyone in it (including, I note with a sigh of compassion, the bad people who really didn't deserve it).

As in Harry's story, these other understandings of the death and resurrection of Jesus move us away from the widespread notion that somebody had to die to pay for the problem of sin, and thank God that Jesus decided to take our place so that we could be redeemed. In looking at Jesus' death and resurrection as God's gracious movement in the world, as God's final victory over the powers of sin and death, we glimpse a different model of salvation than approaching an angry God under the white flag of Jesus' sacrificial death. If God is love, then God will act in love. And if God wishes to destroy the separation between ourselves and God, between ourselves and the rest of creation, between ourselves and our selves, then this will come as an act of love, not an act of justice. So when N. T. Wright says that what happened to Jesus "set in motion the Creator's plan to rescue the world and put it back to rights," and that we all can now be involved in that plan that Jesus set in motion, we are returning to the idea of faith as journey and relationship.[5]

Christianity 2.0 also reminds us that the death and resurrection of Jesus represent a victory over the last gasp of earthly power, as embodied in the Roman Empire, the world's greatest in that era. Through the Roman government, hate, greed, violence, and death did their worst to Jesus. The Romans made him a prisoner; they taunted and tortured him. With his execution, it certainly looked as though they had won. But God's message of love, hope, and reconciliation could not be confined to the grave. The accounts of the risen Christ display a God who was showing the powers of the world that the wellspring of life could not be silenced, that the kingdom of God would come on earth as it had in heaven.

In the relationship model, salvation doesn't ignore sin; the apostle Paul's warning that "all have sinned and come short of the glory of God" (Romans 3:23 KJV, a much-quoted verse among evangelical

Christians) remains true. In our human desires, we are constantly wishing for things that don't last rather than for the things of God. But Jesus' death and resurrection have shown us that the things that don't last also include sin, violence, separation, and death. Because Jesus died and was raised again, all who follow Jesus are freed to become a part of that mission, God's rescue mission for creation. More on this later.

Christians also say frequently that salvation has ramifications for our life to come—that is, for what happens to us after we die; in a later chapter (10) we'll talk more on the end of the world and life after death. But a thoughtful understanding of Christianity demands that we recognize that God's rescue effort is also (and maybe even mostly) concerned with the here and now, and we are called to begin participating in this essential work.

To do that, we join with others who have also enlisted in God's rescue operation—a gathering of Jesus followers from around the globe that we call the church.

For Further Discussion

1. How would you define "sin"? What are some acts or failures to act that you would definitely consider to be sinful? What things do other people consider sinful that you would refuse to regard as sins?
2. Do you believe that humans are naturally drawn toward sin? If so, is that because we are born sinful, or because we choose sin? Do we have the power to choose not to be sinful?
3. When you hear a Christian use the word "saved," what does that mean to you? Do you believe that human beings require salvation? Is salvation individual, communal, or involving all of creation?
4. Why is Jesus' crucifixion so important? What theological understandings have you heard about Jesus' death and resurrection? What ideas do you hold about the story that Jesus died and was raised from the dead?
5. Some Christians argue for a metaphorical understanding of the events of the death and resurrection, some for a literal understanding. Does it matter whether Jesus was bodily raised from

the dead? Can one be a Christian without believing in some sense in the resurrection of Jesus Christ?

For Further Reflection and Study

Marcus J. Borg, *The Heart of Christianity: Rediscovering a Life of Faith* (San Francisco: HarperSanFrancisco, 2003). Borg's wise and accessible book on progressive Christianity contains a chapter on sin and salvation concluding that salvation "is about life with God, life in the presence of God, now and forever." It's a sane and generous account of what disordered desire does to humans, and how God works to overcome it.

John Dominic Crossan and N. T. Wright, *The Resurrection of Jesus*, ed. Robert B. Stewart (Minneapolis: Fortress Press, 2004). Two leading Bible scholars debate the meaning of the death and resurrection of Jesus Christ. Both agree, ultimately, that whether the resurrection is factual or metaphorical, all Christians should, in some way, be changed by it as the redemptive event at the heart of our faith.

Luke Timothy Johnson, *Living Jesus: Learning the Heart of the Gospel* (San Francisco: HarperSanFrancisco, 1999). In this study of the Gospels, Johnson writes that belief in the resurrected Christ should lead us to powerful spiritual understandings. Thinking of Jesus as someone living, rather than someone long dead, will allow us to participate in an unfolding story.

Walter Wink, *Unmasking the Powers: The Invisible Forces That Determine Human Existence* (Philadelphia: Fortress Press, 1986). Part two of a theological trilogy, *Unmasking the Powers* takes a hard look at sin and evil—and at the concept of Satan—to explore the powers that drive us to sin and suggest ways to confront these spiritual forces.

Chapter 8

Ecclesia

The People of God

> **Major Ideas**
> 1. What the church is.
> 2. Why the church matters.
> 3. How to live in Christian community.

Several years ago, I received a small magnet as a premium for making a donation to a left-wing political Web site I frequent. It makes me laugh, and since it would get lost on my refrigerator, I put it on the metal door of my apartment at the Seminary of the Southwest, so that I could not leave the house without seeing it.

The magnet bears the image of a corporate 1950s drone, one of those outdoor-grilling dads we associate with squareness and conformity. This guy is apparently asking our Lord: "Please, Jesus, save me from your followers!"

When we refer back to the upsetting things that people think about Christianity—often with justification—these perceptions seem to be in response to the way Christianity is being lived out in contemporary society (or to be fair, in response to the dominant perceptions concerning that living out). The problem is us, the followers; the problem is not Jesus. Earlier I suggested that people respect and even revere Jesus, the founder of the faith, as well they might. But when they come face-to-face with strident, intolerant, fractious, and/ or narrowly political Christians, they get a vision that frankly doesn't match how Christian life is supposed to be lived. It seems clear that often the ecclesia (from the Greek *ekklēsia*, an assembly or gathering, and frequently translated as "church" in the Christian [or New] Testament) is not representing Jesus well, and for many people, it has actually become an absolute barrier to their desire to know Jesus and his teachings better, let alone live a life of faith.

The prominent Bible scholar Walter Brueggemann wrote recently on this phenomenon, the church that drives people away from Jesus:

You might think

- if you cringe at the boisterous, cocky new sound of religion in politics,
- if you worry about the divisiveness of "red" and "blue," and
- if you are vexed that too many people claim to be speaking directly for Christ, . . .

you might think that our Christian faith is all about getting the moral issues right and leveraging others to think and act the right way, as do we. But if you think that, you are very wrong, because such contemporary loud posturing is not so much about faith as it is about anxiety and maintaining control.[1]

If you've observed the stridency of moral debates, you might indeed think that Christians only care about getting things right—knowing how to act or believe to assure our own salvation, and separating ourselves from anyone else who believes differently. Certainly even the most progressive of the faithful fight among ourselves as though certainty is what matters most, although David Dark argues that most of us are guilty of "selective fundamentalism," surrounding ourselves with people who believe as we do and shutting out dissenting voices.[2] I certainly am. But in this chapter, we're going to put together everything we've learned so far, and I'm going to argue that being a follower of Christ is not centered on certainty. It's not primarily concerned with that single moment of decision we discussed, but with faithful journeying within a countercultural community that tries to live out the redemptive will of God for the world. There are, thanks be to God, individual ecclesias living out this vision in the larger church, which sometimes seems to have lost its way; I've seen them, and perhaps you have too.

Because Christianity 1.0 seems to be caught up in strife over how we interpret the Bible and whether to ordain women and gays, it's hard to see past it to the good being done and the lives being changed in many Christian churches and traditions. In fact, sometimes it's hard to know if good *is* being done and lives *are* being changed, since so much energy is being wasted on contention.

So perhaps to outsiders it does look as though—to paraphrase the magnet on my door—the church is a scary group of Jesus followers from whom people might need protection. But before we talk about "the church," it might be useful to do a little background work for those who don't have a sense of history or an organizational chart handy. It's easy to get lost or misled whenever we say "the church" or "Christendom" as though it's just a religious Walmart, one brand with a number of individual stores in various locations. Without a sense of history, it's even easier to misunderstand our present difficulties. Here's an example of what I mean: When I was growing up, my pastor taught my congregation that the Southern Baptist Church (an American denomination that grew out of the Protestant Reformation, a sixteenth-century rebellion against the excesses of the Roman Catholic Church) had existed for two thousand years in an unbroken line going back to the first Baptist, John the Baptist (who was not, mind you, even Christian, since that term comes along later).

I'd like to think he was joking, but whenever he was joking, he always paused for the laugh.

If leaders inside the tradition can be this unaware of facts, then why should we expect people from outside the tradition to know any better?

But the history of the church does make a difference in how we think about the church, so I want you first to understand that Christianity is not monolithic. All Christians are not alike, so don't smack *me* if a Lutheran once made you mad.

And despite some rumblings to the contrary, Christians have *never* been all alike. Contemporary historical scholarship into the beginnings of the Christian church shows that Jesus' early followers banded together around quite different understandings of the Jesus story (hence the different Gospels, which were normative in each community), and that the myth of a single and cohesive church planted by Jesus and coming down to us in unbroken succession is just that, a myth, if a beautiful one. Jesus, as we've noted earlier, was an observant Jew who did not come to found a new religion, although his followers found it impossible to remain within the Jewish tradition. Jesus' teachings and the story of his wondrous life, death, and resurrection gradually spilled out into the non-Jewish world, where it took hold and spread.

So while we might think of the Catholic Church, say, as carrying a long history (and devout Catholics themselves may believe that those claiming to be Christian outside the confines of their tradition are just fooling themselves), the institutional church has not existed in any clear and unbroken line for two thousand years. It took its own sweet time wrestling with doctrine and worship, gradually weeding out heretical (that is, unorthodox) beliefs, and around 313 the bishop of Rome began to assume primacy over the other bishops of the church so that what we now recognize as the Holy Roman Church came into being.

But even given this primacy and the monolithic nature of the Roman Church, there were early dissenting traditions (although their members were sometimes burned alive as fiery warnings against dissent). Among the heretical groups, the Coptic Church in Egypt, the Eastern Orthodox tradition, and the proliferation of traditions stemming from the Protestant Reformation five hundred years ago, today we find ourselves living with a strange polyglot mix of Christians. There are nondenominational megachurches and cowboy churches and biker churches and house churches as well as that denominational church on the corner that changes its sign out front every week, although the message nonetheless always seems to suggest that anyone not believing what its members believe will be getting the devil's suntan.

So when we say "the church," we can't say that there's now (or for much of history, ever has been) one representative version, although outsiders do tend to lump all Christians together and start making negative assumptions about them because of their least favorite contacts with the faith, whether that was with Catholics or Pentecostals or Quakers.

But what we can generalize about individual churches is this: whether or not they like to admit it, all are part of the worldwide church, what the Bible calls "the body of Christ" or, using a different metaphor, "the bride of Christ." In some statements like the Nicene Creed, Christians express their belief in this universal faith— "We believe in one holy, catholic, and apostolic church"—a phrase that has often stuck in the throats of non-Catholics, although it's not referring to the Roman Church. "Catholic" comes from the Greek *katholikos*, meaning "universal," so the creed simply recognizes the reality of the entire body of Christ, testifying to one faith (even as we acknowledge here how that faith has split into myriad minifaiths).

But although the idea some outsiders have concerning a mono-lithic Christianity is wrong, it does lead us in the direction of at least one thing that is right: all Christians belong to a single movement. Christians from around the world, past and present, are members of the body of Christ, doing the work he began during his time on earth. Unfortunately, Christians often don't recognize this, sometimes they refuse to think of themselves as part of something any larger than their local community of faith, than the like-minded believers gath-ered to left and right.

That, I think, is tragic.

It's a particular problem in America, where our emphases on self-reliance and individuality have refashioned Christianity into a consumer-driven faith that one can opt out of when it impinges a little too much on cherished freedoms. There's an old joke in the Baptist Church (although it seems to apply to every other Christian tradition short of the Roman Catholic Church) that misquotes a verse from the Gospel of Matthew (18:20) to make its point: "Whenever two or more Baptists are gathered together, one of them is going off to start a new church."

We can find plenty of examples of this in my current tradition, the Episcopal Church of the United States of America (ECUSA), where some congregations and even some large administrative dis-tricts called dioceses have split away from the national church in the past few decades over questions of church authority, ordina-tion of women, gays in the church, and proper worship. These splits are nothing new within the Episcopal Church. Just a few blocks from where my ex-girlfriend lives in Austin is a congregation that refused to give up the 1928 Book of Common Prayer when the national denomination introduced a revised prayer book in 1979. Its aging members will live out their remaining years listening to the comfortable liturgies, sure that they have done the right thing in withdrawing all those years ago from the Diocese of Texas and the ECUSA, but split from their tradition and from their larger Christian identity.

So it is and has been and will be, I'm sure. People split away from churches and denominations because of personality issues, theological disagreements, divergent musical tastes, or because they think their wording of the prayer of confession is the only one that God hears. Not all of these splits are bad things, and God has used some of them for great good. But this insistence on being right and on not associating with those who are wrong (whether coming from the left or the right) represents disaster for the reality of the larger church. If Christians can't demonstrate their love for other Christians, then how—in the name of all that is holy—can witnesses from outside the tradition understand that Christians are supposed to bear a message of love and reconciliation?

When I asked the bishop of Texas, Andy Doyle, to identify the greatest problem facing the church, he said it was this splintering of the body of Christ into smaller and more-divided units at the same time that the church hopes to reach out to a broken world. "We are a house divided against itself," he said, "and yet we're trying to reach a population that comes out of divorce and broken families who don't want to enter that broken system again." And honestly, who could blame them? It's one thing to say that God is love, which I believe. But how can anyone be introduced to that God of love by an institution that doesn't exemplify love, whose members vilify those who disagree with them, or who simply pull away from them—choosing divorce, to use Bishop Doyle's image, instead of reconciliation?

But it doesn't have to be that way, as Bishop Doyle affirms: "One model for how we might relate to each other is the realization that you don't have to leave the table. It would be nice if we could get away from the idea that I have to be right." This would be a shift into privileging practice and community, rather than doctrine or dogma. Some ecclesias in the Episcopal Church (and in the Presbyterian, Baptist, and Catholic traditions, among others) are living out this vision amid the church's fragmentation.

Many of those fissures have emerged from an insistence on being doctrinally correct. But such fragmentation can be averted when faith communities embrace tolerance, ambiguity, and the understanding that we are ill placed to know the exact will of God or the only possible interpretation of Holy Scripture. David Dark reports that his own faith journey became authentic and life-giving when "Christianity—far from being a tradition in which doubts and questions are suppressed in favor of uncritical, blind faith, began to assume the form of a robust culture in which anything can be asked and anything can be said."[3] Or to return to his earlier idea, perhaps real Christianity can emerge wherever churches stop being filled with selective fundamentalists of whatever stripe.

Jesus himself, in imagining the communities that would form around his teaching and actions, left only a handful of rules. Some of them grew out of the Jewish tradition from which he came. Instead of the endless qualifications some contemporary Christian communities create that identify people within them as saved or damned, Jesus relied on ancient formulations: the Ten Commandments, the requirement that the faithful love God with all they have and their neighbors as themselves. These ideas weren't surprising to those who heard them, although they might seem surprising now; the parable of the Good Samaritan remains a jarring reminder that we are supposed to help even those who differ conspicuously from us, that we are not allowed to pick and choose our neighbors based on whether they look or act or believe like we do. As Walter Brueggemann points out, the church exists in large part to reach out to those who are least like ourselves.[4]

In the Gospel of Matthew, the only Gospel where the word "ecclesia" appears, Jesus commands members of the church to forgive each other and seek ways to keep from splintering their fellowship even when one of them has wronged others. In the Gospel of John, Jesus leaves the commandment that his followers love each other as he has loved them, and he reminds them that no greater love exists than to give your life for those you love.

We sometimes hear these passages of the Bible on forgiveness, reconciliation, and love selectively, for if we took them seriously, how could Christians allow themselves to splinter the body of Christ into so many pieces?

Moreover, if we took seriously the idea of working out our salvation with other believers, how could Americans have slipped so deeply into the heretical belief that our individual salvation is the most important thing about our faith?

I recently read a paper on the African concept of *ubuntu* by a seminary student from the southwestern African country of Namibia. She explored an idea she knew from her childhood that has been widely discussed in recent years by Desmond Tutu, the archbishop of South Africa. Unlike American understandings of the autonomous self that have led to heresies such as the extreme emphasis on our personal salvation, Africans understand that we are formed and shaped in community, and that we need each other to become all we are called to be, particularly including faithful Christians. Ubuntu means that, as John Donne wrote, "No man is an island, entire of himself," and that as Bono sang, "We get to carry each other."

And it means that if we focus solely on how we have Jesus as our own personal Lord and Savior, we ignore the great web of connectivity that we find in the Christian tradition—going back to the Jewish tradition from which Jesus came.

As we look at the narrative of salvation, it begins with God asking a man named Abram to make a choice—an individual choice of the salvation and divine blessing that will come into the world through the descendants of Abram (later Abraham). It's a blessing to and through a people instead of a single individual:

> Now the LORD said to Abram, "Go from your country and your kindred and your father's house to the land that I will show you. I will make of you a great nation, and I will bless you, and make your name great, so that you will be a blessing. I will bless those who bless you, and the one who curses you I will curse; and in you all the families of the earth shall be blessed." (Genesis 12:1–3)

This chosen people, the Jews, are made up of individuals—sometimes notable individuals like Moses or Joshua or David. But God's salvation—his purpose for the world—is being lived out through the entire nation. The Hebrews (later the Israelites) understood that they were part of something larger than themselves, that their worship and faithful practice of God's law occurred in community.

Likewise in the Gospel narratives, Jesus didn't gather a single great man (or great woman) to transmit God's new instructions; he chose a group of people, a set of disciples who would be a core group, even as they were followed around Palestine by a larger group of disciples. And again, while Jesus—like God the Father—asked individuals to make hard decisions on their priorities, the story of Jesus' life and ministry takes place communally, among a group of imperfect but willing disciples. Writer and Jesus follower Anne Lamott once told me, "I don't know why God picks cowards and mealy-mouths and narcissists to carry his word. But he does, and he always has." And it is in this gathering of cowards and narcissists, the imperfect but willing, that we will find ourselves when we are doing Christianity as Jesus suggested.

It's true that our redemption revolves around an individual decision. We have to turn away from the selfish story that the world—and sometimes even American Christianity—tries to tell us we ought to be living. But a journey of faith is only real when we are journeying alongside others, bouncing off their opinions, coming to new understandings, offending and being offended, forgiving and being forgiven, shaping and being shaped by others.

It's a challenging vision. It's much more demanding than the illusion that we can rest secure in our own salvation while the rest of the world literally or metaphorically goes to hell.

But that's what ecclesia—or church—means.

Church is not singing hymns or choruses or listening to Anglican chant; it's not dressing up or dressing down to attend a service. It's not a building, if your ecclesia has one, even if we call that building a church. All of those things, comforting or inspiring as we may sometimes find them, are not the point of faith. You can know every word in every service in the Presbyterian Book of Worship or all the words in all seven verses of "Just As I Am," and it won't mean you're a faithful Christian.

Ecclesia is the messy and imperfect and nonetheless beautiful body of Christ that God has called us to be part of by calling us to God. Desmond Tutu has written that God has a dream that "My children will know that they are members of one family, the human family, God's family, My family."[5] The sooner we realize that we're called to be a part of something so much larger than ourselves, the sooner we can get down to what Christians are supposed to be doing. And that is helping God redeem the world, so that everyone knows—so that people can see with their own eyes—that they are meant to be a part of God's family as well.

For Further Discussion

1. People often have widely varied experiences with the concept of church. Have you had negative experiences with churches? Positive experiences? What are your most vivid memories of church?
2. If you're not a Jesus follower, would you say that you have in your head an impression that all Christians are alike? If so, how? If not, what differences have you observed? If you are a follower of Christ, do you like or resent being asked if you are Christian? What fears—or hopes—run through your mind at that question?
3. Have you noticed any examples in your own life or faith tradition of the "selective fundamentalism" that David Dark describes? What things do you consider to be so important (political, religious, philosophical, or otherwise) that you prefer to be around people who will not challenge your beliefs? What would it feel like to dialogue with someone who had a different opinion?
4. What do you think the phrase "Jesus Christ is my personal Lord and Savior" means? Is this a phrase you would feel comfortable using? Why or why not?
5. Arguing that individuals are saved in Christian community instead of individually sounds countercultural. Do you prefer this Western/American idea that individual faith or belief is most important, or do you find wisdom in the African concept of *ubuntu*, that without community we cannot be our true selves?

For Further Reflection and Study

Diana Butler Bass, *A People's History of Christianity: The Other Side of the Story* (San Francisco: HarperOne, 2009). Bass explores the history of the church from the standpoint of common people and finds that faith, hope, and love are Christianity's real traditions.

Marcus Borg and John Dominic Crossan, *The First Paul: Reclaiming the Radical Visionary behind the Church's Conservative Icon* (San Francisco: HarperOne, 2009). Borg and Crossan argue that the apostle Paul's primary concern was not with individual salvation, but with creating new Christ-following communities that illustrated God's great cleanup of the world.

Desmond Tutu, *God Has a Dream: A Vision of Hope for Our Time* (New York: Doubleday/Image, 2004). When Desmond Tutu speaks of his faith, he is speaking out of a life that bears striking moral witness, so his image of a faith in which there are no outsiders, in which everyone shares in God's love and the awareness of God's blessing, becomes compelling for the church.

L. Michael White, *From Jesus to Christianity* (San Francisco: HarperSanFrancisco, 2004). Scholar Michael White walks us through the diverse groups in the first four generations of Jesus followers to introduce us to the progress of the faith from a backwater belief held by strikingly different groups in the years just after Jesus died to a movement that spread throughout the Roman Empire by the end of the second century.

Chapter 9

The Kingdom of God

Major Ideas

1. How heaven and the kingdom of God differ.
2. What Jesus taught about the kingdom of God.
3. How we participate in the kingdom of God.

*J*esus tells numerous stories in the Gospels about something called the kingdom of heaven or the kingdom of God or the reign of God—something he says, tantalizingly, is coming close even as he speaks. It's a puzzling idea—or at least it has puzzled people for two thousand years so far. Many American Christians understand it as pertaining to salvation, heaven, and life after death. I think that when Jesus sees us deciding that, he shakes his head sadly and wonders if maybe he should have hired a leading PR firm to get out his message instead of telling all those parables.

I'd like to retell a story that Brian McLaren shares in his book *The Secret Message of Jesus.* It is a parable of sorts, the same kind of story that Jesus used to relate. Imagine, Brian says, if Jesus were around today, preaching and teaching and trying to share his message of the kingdom of God. What if Jesus were to sit down street-side with a TV reporter at a coffee shop to share what he's here to do?

Jesus starts out by telling her stories, just like he does in the Gospels: "The kingdom of heaven is like a mustard seed that a farmer sowed in his field, the tiniest seed we know, but it grows up into a tree that the birds can roost in." "The kingdom of heaven is like finding treasure hidden in a field, treasure so precious that you sell everything you have and buy that field." And so on.

"Enough with this kingdom of heaven thing already," the reporter finally says. "Why can't you just tell me what you're all about?"

She takes a puff from her cigarette, coughs a little too hard, a little too long. "I wish I could give these damn things up," she sighs when she sees that Jesus looks concerned. "I can't seem to stop. And now I'm worried—"

And then she coughs some more.

"Would you like to be healed of that cough?" Jesus asks.

"Sure," she laughs. "And why don't you get rid of this nicotine addiction while you're at it?"

"Okay," Jesus says, and he smiles. Then he leans forward. "Do you believe that God is in the healing business?"

"Oh," she says. "Religion. I—well, theoretically, I guess. But I don't really have much faith—"

"All you need is a little," Jesus says to her. "You're healed."

In that instant, she realizes that her cough is gone. More than that, her impulse to smoke has also completely disappeared.

She pulls in a deep breath, lets it out, and realizes that her lungs have not felt so full and healthy in years.

"That is a tiny taste of the kingdom of God," Jesus tells her.

He lays some money on the table, gets up, and walks off.[1]

A tiny taste of the kingdom of God. That's what we're discussing in this chapter, and it's the ultimate destination for the church. The kingdom is the culmination of all those pilgrimages we imagined that people might take, of the faith and expectation that the Jesus followers have had for two thousand years, even if not all of them recognized or even understood that this is what they were hoping for.

If, as we said in the chapter (7) on sin and salvation, we could think of God not as some kind of cosmic sadist or as judge, jury, and executioner, but rather as the loving God of new life, then maybe this story makes sense. Jesus, God's best answer to all of our questions, walked around healing, teaching, and practicing a faith that had nothing to do with buying into wealth and power.

This faith in God had nothing to do with what was best for Jesus, who wound up beaten, spat upon, tortured, and executed.

But it had everything to do with loving and serving and gathering people together to work for the healing of the world.

When Jesus came, he told people that he was giving them a tiny taste of the kingdom of God, of the good that God had in mind for all of creation if we were willing to accept it, to get down in the trenches and work to bring it closer.

However, we've substituted a bad salvation story that has gotten in the way of that all-encompassing kingdom. Too many people think that Jesus came to save them from hell when that is only a minuscule part of what God had in mind for us.

Yes, God wants us to be in eternal relationship with him, and yes, as Rowan Williams has said, God has no intention to abandon what he has created and redeemed.[2] In the next chapter we'll talk more about heaven and hell, after we've reordered our priorities a bit. Too much preoccupation with the afterlife removes our focus from the here and now.

Brian McLaren's book says that the secret message of Jesus is not the secret of eternal life, or how to get out of hell free (like one of those marquee signs I saw outside a church offering "Son screen"), and the secret certainly isn't that Jesus was married to Mary Magdalene and his great-grandkid may have delivered your paper this morning, whatever Dan Brown might have told you.

The secret message of Jesus, taught in Jesus' roundabout fashion and symbolized by the healing and feeding miracles, was the still-dangerous message that the things of this world are not God. Only God is worthy of our worship and investment. We are called to get on board with God's program of healing and reconciliation, even though it might unsettle people who have made idols of power, wealth, or acclaim. As Brian describes it, the secret message is that the kingdom of God is revolutionary, countercultural, "proclaiming a ceaseless rebellion against the tyrannical trinity of money, sex, and power" so the things that matter can emerge into view.[3]

This sounds like a very different thing than salvation, redemption, or any of those other religious buzzwords that religious people sometimes hang around themselves like the "flair" that waitrons are supposed to wear in the cult film *Office Space*. In that movie, the waitress played by Jennifer Aniston is told that what is important in her job has almost nothing to do with her real job—that wearing cheerful buttons matters more than giving customers cheerful service. In a similar way, we have gotten lost in hanging the language of individual redemption upon ourselves so that we have become focused on it instead of what it's supposed to point us toward—a life lived in service to a redeeming God. Stanley Hauerwas explains it in this way:

> The language of creation and redemption, nature and grace, is a secondary theological language, that is sometimes mistaken for the story itself. . . . That God "saves" is not a pietistic claim about my status individually. . . . The God of Israel and Jesus offers us salvation insofar as we are invited to become citizens of the kingdom and thus to be participants in the history which God is creating.[4]

In other words, salvation is included in the deal, but it is not the deal itself.

I am not the center of the universe, as I am reminded by my kids, my students, and life in general. So why should my individual salvation matter so much, anyway?

This, then, is the truth: it doesn't. Except as it is part of God's larger plan of saving everyone and everything, of redeeming all of creation, my salvation is not the point of the kingdom of God.

In the chapter (4) on the Bible and theology, we saw that the Bible seems to convey God's plan for creation, starting with the fact that God cared enough to create it at all. After that he designated a group of people, the Jews, to be his chosen people and a blessing to the entire world. Later he sent prophets to call those chosen people back to right worship and right behavior, which includes faith in the One God and care for those who have little: the widows, orphans, and aliens (that is, strangers) among them.

And finally, we believe, there was Jesus, who was God's walking, talking billboard for his plan of action. Jesus proclaimed forgiveness of sins and debts, healed the blind and crippled and sick, and fed the hungry. He associated with the outcasts of his society, not with the moneyed elite, the right thinkers, or the powers that be.

And when Jesus taught his followers how to pray, he used a deeply Jewish prayer that seems focused on this world:

> Pray then in this way:
> Our Father in heaven,
>   hallowed be your name.
>   Your kingdom come.
>   Your will be done,
>   on earth as it is in heaven.
>   Give us this day our daily bread.
>   And forgive us our debts,
>   as we also have forgiven our debtors.
>   And do not bring us to the time of trial,
>   but rescue us from the evil one.
>   (Matthew 6:9–13)

Notice that in this model prayer, there's not much on being saved for the next life. Jesus' prayer homes in on this life: forgiveness of debts in a world where many struggle under the weight of obligation, bread for the many who go hungry, and arching over it all, this request: "Your will be done, on earth as it is in heaven."

We're praying for your plan, God, to go to work here, now, with us.

This Lord's Prayer, as it is famously known, shows us a vision of God's plan: it calls for the kingdom of God that we've been discussing (which is not heaven, as is sometimes mistakenly thought—don't skip ahead to the next chapter, I beg you) to come on earth. In calling for this kingdom, Jesus delivers what Jewish New Testament scholar Amy-Jill Levine describes as a slap in the face of this world, a rebuke to all the broken or misplaced passions and powers. As we see in this prayer and in his other teachings, for Jesus, the kingdom of Heaven is not "a piece of real estate of the single saved soul; it is a communal vision of what could be and what should be, . . . a vision of a time when all debts are forgiven, when we stop judging others, when we not only wear our traditions on our sleeve, but also hold them in our hearts and minds and enact them with all our strength."[5]

Jesus calls for us to be part of this plan, which incidentally but not centrally offers us God's grace and redemption for our own broken and misguided selves. But how? As we saw in our chapter (4) on the Bible, people tease all sorts of meanings out of the text. How do we know what we're supposed to be doing to participate in God's rescue effort?

When in doubt, look at Jesus. In focusing his ministry on the outcast, sick, demon possessed, and all those on the margins of society, Jesus was living out God's call to repair the world at its most broken places. A few years ago, U2's Bono spoke at the President's Prayer Breakfast, an annual interfaith event in Washington, D.C., and there issued his standard call for religious accountability:

> God may well be with us in our mansions on the hill. . . . I hope so. He may well be with us in all manner of controversial stuff . . . maybe, maybe not. But the one thing on which we can all agree, among all faiths and ideologies, is that God is with the vulnerable and the poor. God is in the slums, in the cardboard boxes where the poor play house. God is in the silence of a mother who has infected her child with a virus that will end both their lives. God is in the cries heard under the rubble of war. God is in the debris of wasted opportunity and lives, and God is with us if we are with them.[6]

So, Bono reminds us, our task is to be with those who are broken. The places where things are broken are where God is at work. And that means climbing down from our positions of privilege. (Unless you are one of the homeless, reading this book in a public library or after fishing it out of a dumpster, you are privileged; even the most menially employed American enjoys a higher standard of living than almost anyone in the world.) It means working alongside and for the benefit of those who have little or nothing, pushing back against prejudice and systems that exalt some at the expense of others, and trying to repair the damage that we've done to creation itself. To work for the kingdom of God, paying attention to Jesus' example, is to work for reconciliation and refuse to be complicit with the forces that degrade and pervert humanity.

During the Middle Ages, the faithful were entertained and edified by a kind of literature we now call "saints' lives," a recounting of miracles, good deeds, and often martyrdoms, intended to provide an example for Christians to follow. In contemporary life, kingdom work has taken tangible form in the lives of many modern-day saints who instruct and inspire us.

I nominate for sainthood Dorothy Day (1897–1980), a Catholic writer and reformer who created a network of urban living spaces where the faithful lived alongside and served the poor. She was an advocate for the rights of exploited workers everywhere, and she spoke out for peace in a culture of violence and war. In the Catholic Worker movement, which Day founded with Peter Maurin, the poor are still being cared for—and those who are more affluent are blessed by their work with the poor.

I also nominate the Rev. Dr. Martin Luther King Jr. (1929–68). He was a Baptist preacher and theologian whose comfortable black middle-class existence became uncomfortable in 1958, when he was asked to lead a bus boycott in segregated Montgomery, Alabama, to protest racist policies on public transportation. His preaching took on a new character: "God is at work in his universe," he said; "he is striving in our striving."[7] In the course of his assassin-shortened life of preaching and prayer and activism, King took on business interests, government policies, war, hunger, and prejudice. By sharing his dream that someday color would matter less than a person's character, he predicted a more equitable world that we are now—maybe, please God—starting to realize.

I nominate the Presbyterian preacher and rabble-rouser the Rev. Dr. William Sloane Coffin (1924–2006). Coffin, like his contemporary Dr. King, spoke out against the Vietnam War, against a culture of empire, and against all the forces of this world that stand in the way of our doing God's kingdom work. He did so with an energy and eloquence that not even death could silence. His famous blessing—long before I knew these were his words—rang with truth for me whenever my friend John Ballenger would use it to conclude a service: "The world is now too dangerous for anything but truth and too small for anything but love."

I nominate Archbishop Oscar Romero (1917–80), a conservative Catholic who had the audacity to discover the needs, desires, and fears of the people he served in El Salvador. When he could easily have sat the battle out, Romero became a force for justice, speaking against the violence he saw being carried out by people on both the right and the left. He became an advocate for the poor and powerless despite threats against his life, aligning the Roman Catholic Church in El Salvador with all those struggling for peace and justice. In response to the violence that ultimately martyred him in the very act of celebrating the Mass, Romero once said, "A murdered priest is a testimonial of a church incarnate in the problems of the people."[8] And so it was—and is.

And I nominate Dr. Lisa Y. Sullivan (1961–2001), an African American community organizer in Washington, D.C., who earned a PhD from Yale but felt called to the streets and to forgotten children of every hue. Sullivan worked for the Children's Defense Fund and served on the board of the Christian peace and justice organization called Sojourners. She died young of heart disease, but is often remembered now by her friend Jim Wallis: When people would complain, as they do, that there are no saints out there to lead us, "Lisa would get angry. 'We are the ones we have been waiting for!' she would declare. Lisa was a person of faith. And hers was a powerful call to leadership and responsibility and a deep affirmation of hope."[9]

You may remember that "We are the ones we have been waiting for" was also a call to action used by Barack Obama in his 2008 presidential campaign, but this call goes well beyond politics. To imagine that religion is not political is to deny that it has a public element. Salvation-centered faith can remain private (although, paradoxically, it often doesn't), but kingdom-centered faith cannot. If Jesus is—as we affirm—Lord, then that affirmation will dethrone everything else. That confession will be acted out in the entirety of our lives, private and public, political and economic. It might lead us to do some of the following:

- Build homes with others in Habitat for Humanity.
- Cook and serve food for the homeless in a soup kitchen, or stock shelves in a food bank.
- Speak out, march, and write against violence and war.
- Work for public policies that extend health care, decent jobs, housing, and dignity to those who desperately need them.
- Adopt orphans, provide foster care, or sponsor those who do.
- Offer hospitality and compassion to the strangers among us, including those who are unlike us and even those who despise us.
- Give of our own resources to those who are less fortunate.
- Use fewer resources, so that this creation we share with others will be less tortured by pollution, garbage, and climate change; and thereby save creation, which God has called good and beautiful.

In none of this should these actions become our new gods. We are not replacing obsession with our own individual salvation with, say, obsession over recycling #2 plastics. Nor should we make the mistake of believing that by taking part in these actions we are saving ourselves. The apostle Paul said in his Letters that we are not redeemed by anything we do, but through the grace of God, and this is true. But as James writes, works are also an essential part of a faithful life:

> What good is it, my brothers and sisters, if you say you have faith but do not have works? Can faith save you? If a brother or sister is naked and lacks daily food, and one of you says to them, "Go in peace; keep warm and eat your fill," and yet you do not supply their bodily needs, what is the good of that? So faith by itself, if it has no works, is dead.
>
> But someone will say, "You have faith and I have works." Show me your faith apart from your works, and I by my works will show you my faith. (James 2:14–18)

When we are called to work for the coming of God's kingdom, to throw our backs into God's plan for the cosmos, we are working from that perspective of faith; working in imitation of Jesus, who is our great model of that faith; and working with each other, so that we can pray for and support each other in this work that the world itself resists.

And we do it, not because it makes us look good, not simply because it gives us the opportunity to tell other people what we believe, not because we'll get jewels in our heavenly crowns, and not because we'll go to hell if we don't.

We join in working for God's kingdom because that is what Christians are called to do.

For Further Discussion

1. Judging from the behavior of Christians you know, what is the purpose of Christianity? Is it gaining eternal life? Doing good works? Refraining from evil?

2. What do you think of when you hear the phrases "kingdom of heaven" or "kingdom of God"? Do you imagine they deal primarily with life after death, or life in this world? Does hearing that they focus on this life change any of your thoughts about what Christians are called to do?
3. How often have you heard the Lord's Prayer? Why do you suppose Jesus offered it as a model prayer?
4. What actions do you feel called to as a result of your faith?
5. Does working for the kingdom have a new meaning for you after reading this chapter? Might this kind of faithful living change some of the negative ways people think about Christians?

For Further Study and Reflection

Dorothy Day, *The Long Loneliness: The Autobiography of Dorothy Day* (San Francisco: HarperSanFrancisco, 1997). In this autobiography, Day tells the stories behind her life—why she felt called to solidarity with marginalized workers and the poor, and how she turned that call into tangible actions on their behalf.

Martin Luther King Jr., *I Have a Dream: Writings and Speeches That Changed the World* (San Francisco: HarperSanFrancisco, 1992). In this collection of Dr. King's best-known speeches, sermons, and essays, we find his passionate and reasoned call to get in line with God's plan by standing against prejudice, poverty, and violence through prayer and public action.

Brian D. McLaren, *Everything Must Change: Jesus, Global Crises, and a Revolution of Hope* (Nashville: Thomas Nelson, 2007). McLaren focuses our attention on what it might look like to be followers of Jesus today, and why Christianity is the world's best hope.

Jim Wallis, *God's Politics: Why the Right Gets Its Wrong and the Left Doesn't Get It* (San Francisco: HarperSanFrancisco, 2005). Wallis, the leader of the Sojourners movement, makes a powerful and scriptural case for social action on the part of God's people. Instead of single-issue politics revolving around a chosen moral issue, Wallis argues that "God's politics" is a kingdom politics opposing war, oppression, poverty, and bigotry.

N. T. Wright, *Evil and the Justice of God* (Downers Grove, IL: InterVarsity Press, 2006). In this study of the power and presence of evil in the world, one of the foremost teachers of kingdom Christianity argues that God's ultimate purpose is to rid the world of evil. Rather than relying on the mythical powers of "progress," we are called to prayer, holiness, and some specific biblically centered actions as God's agents.

Chapter 10

The End of Things

Major Ideas
1. Why the end of the world captivates us.
2. How our understandings of the end times have come to be.
3. What the Bible itself teaches about what is coming next.

In every conversation I've had with her for over forty years, my Grandma Irene, one of the world's most faithful Christians, has asked me if I'm living right.

"Are you going to church?" she asks. "Are you reading your Bible?"

Her concern is not for my moral development—or at least, not in the way we've been discussing in this book, as part of an ongoing journey that includes spiritual practice. She's concerned with my immortal soul. In her mind, Jesus is coming again, and it could be any day now. And if I'm not in a good place with God, as evidenced by these particular proofs, then she worries I could wind up in a very hot place.

My grandma, like many American Christians, is quite a scholar of the end of all things. Although she never completed high school, she has a functional PhD in evangelical soteriology (how we are redeemed, from the Greek word *sōtēria*, which means "salvation") and in eschatology (the study of the end, from the Greek *eschatos*, which means "last"). Where prophecy, the rapture, and heaven are concerned, she has read more books, watched more TV programs, and spent more time presenting her conclusions than any religion professor I know. All of it has centered around what for her are the central questions of faith: Where is the world headed? (Answer, by the way: To hell in a handbasket.) And the most important—because most personal—question, which grows out of the first: What will happen to me after this life?

For many Christians—I don't want to say most, although it often seems so, judging from the way Christians are represented in the media—where we will spend eternity, whether in heaven or in hell, drives our faith. Preachers in many traditions offer up hellfire-and-brimstone sermons intended to convince people that the threat of eternity in hell should change their behavior now. "Repent or Perish," read the billboard I saw on I-20 outside of Slidell, Louisiana; "Prepare to meet God!" was a message on I 440 in Arkansas. "Repent, for the end is near!" is at the heart of this understanding of faith. Put simply, it suggests that if we don't change our behavior before the world ends, as it's going to, we're headed for eternal punishment.

My grandmother's conclusions, as well as those of many better-known evangelical eschatologists, are of this sort: disaster is coming, as foretold in the biblical books of Daniel, Ezekiel, Mark, and Revelation; the world as we know it will be destroyed. My grandmother, like many others, believes that Jesus will return and gather his faithful so that they won't be forced to live through the hard final days leading to the final judgment. After that judging of all humankind, the bad will go to the bad place, and the faithful will go to be with God, where they will walk streets of gold, live in mansions, and have crowns with stars in them. Thus I quote again the evangelical hymn "Are You Washed in the Blood": "When the Bridegroom cometh will your robes be white? . . . Will your soul be ready for the mansions bright?"

So Christianity 1.0 tells us that faithful Christians will enjoy white robes and bright mansions for all eternity.

Many Americans—including people who are not particularly religious—have apocalyptic beliefs (from the Greek *apokalypsis*, which means to reveal) concerning the end of the world. British philosopher John Gray argues that Western culture has been haunted by Bible-scented visions of the Apocalypse; Nicholas Guyatt notes that in a 2002 poll commissioned by *Time* and CNN, almost 60 percent of Americans believed that the book of Revelation contains apocalyptic prophecies that will literally come true, with almost 20 percent (representing over fifty million Americans) believing that this apocalypse will happen in their lifetimes.[1] The Left Behind series of novels, which have sold over sixty million copies in all editions, broadcast a belief that Christians will be given an escape hatch from the world's problems via the rapture of the faithful.

The worst practices exemplified by American Christians—a shortsighted focus on individual salvation, a disengagement from the world, a fear or hatred of those who differ from them—finally center around beliefs in the end of the world and life after death. So I think that before we conclude, it's important to wrestle with some popular notions about these things and try to recenter Christian belief and practice where they belong—here on earth. But that can be hard to do when even those Christians who claim to read the Bible promulgate ideas on the end of the world and eternal life that don't seem to be supported by the Bible.

If you have not been part of a faith tradition that endorses the rapture—and many Christians have not been—then you might regard those who believe in it as, well, demented. This view dominates The London *Observer*'s review of Guyatt's book on American apocalyptic faith: "A jaunty report . . . from the front line of wacky religious fervor." But the fact that millions of Americans do believe in a literal rapture of the saints has shaped not just their own religious practice, but also their views on political, social, economic, and environmental issues, as we saw in the last chapter. Barbara Rossing calls the rapture a racket, "a theology that distorts God's vision for the world," proclaiming escape instead of healing, violence and war instead of peace.[2] If the rapture is imminent and Christians are going to be airlifted out of the world's suffering, then what incentive is there to care for anything beyond one's own salvation? We could overfish the seas, drill for oil offshore or in the Arctic wilderness, drive a Hummer, bomb Iraq. None of it matters if we're not going to be around long enough to suffer the consequences.

Let's address some of the issues with the rapture teachings. First, there is no passage in the Bible that spells out the doctrine of the rapture, and even rapture theologians admit that the details of this teaching have to be pieced together from different parts of the Bible.

The teaching itself is not a part of ancient Christian understandings, although the church has long looked for Christ to return. Most scholars date the rapture to the teachings of the nineteenth-century British evangelist John Nelson Darby (1800–1882), who was the founder of the Christian sect called the Plymouth Brethren. Darby is said to have been absorbed by a vision in which a fifteen-year-old girl in Scotland described seeing Christ returning in two stages rather than the one the church had always anticipated. Darby went on to teach that Jesus would first return secretly to take up his church in an event called the rapture. Then after seven years of global horrors that Christians, thankfully, would miss, Jesus would return again to establish his kingdom on earth.

These theories were preserved in the Scofield Reference Bible, a popular King James translation that made repeated references to Darby's teachings. I still have the one I was given as a teen, a red-leather Bible with extensive concordance and chain notes referring to the end of the world. Prophecy enthusiasts, evangelists, and even whole seminaries took up the teaching in the twentieth century, and in recent decades, best-selling works like Hal Lindsey's *The Late Great Planet Earth*, the Left Behind novels, and the books of Texas preacher John Hagee have preserved the theology that this world is in its final days, but that Christians can expect to be shot into the heavens before the worst stuff can happen.

I was taught these doctrines from my childhood and was frankly terrified by them. What if I wasn't gathered up with the other Christians? What if I returned from school and the rest of my family was gone? (On more than one occasion I came home to an empty or seemingly empty house and started looking around for evidence of the rapture—clothes fallen in untidy piles, for example, although I didn't have to look any further than my own room for that.) In church we sang plenty of songs about the end times, but I remember particularly "I Wish We'd All Been Ready," a moody, spooky song about how the King has come and gone, "and you've been left behind."

Now none of this is to say that God couldn't order the end of things this way if God chose to, and it certainly is not to say that despite my own fear and trembling, Christians have not received some solace from these readings of Daniel and Revelation for the past 180 years or so. Apocalyptic literature—even if it's made up—has always brought comfort to people who feel that while they're on the inside, terrible things are happening just outside. Apocalyptic stories tell us that God's judgment approaches, but if we are on God's side, we will be saved. They remind people that although the world can be confusing, frightening, and chaotic, ultimately God is in control of all things. God is going to set things right, the faithful will be rewarded, and any present sorrows will be forgotten in the wake of God's powerful rearrangement of the game board.

So it's no wonder that the strange and hallucinogenic Revelation to John, as the book of Revelation is sometimes called, has pervaded fantasies, fears, and hopes about approaching apocalypse, and has become a meaning-making narrative for most of us in the West, Christian and secular alike. As Jonathan Kirsch writes in a book with the grandiose but accurate subtitle *How the Most Controversial Book in the Bible Changed the Course of Western Civilization*, "Revelation is always present, sometimes in plain sight and sometimes just beneath the surface."[3]

For two thousand years the apocalyptic ideas communicated in Revelation have shaped the way we live, believe, vote, and are entertained, even if it has done so for the wrong reasons. Some groups of Christians have always employed the book as a guide to the end of the world, assuming that John, the purported receiver of Revelation, was given prophetic knowledge of the future, which he shared with his hearers in coded symbolic language. Yet according to Raymond Brown, Christian scholars do not imagine that Revelation predicts the future except in the most general and faithful sense. Revelation expresses for believers "an absolute conviction that God would triumph by saving those who remained loyal and by defeating the forces of evil."[4] But the details of this triumph—the exact date, place, and time of some apocalyptic moment—were not and could not be known from the prophetic sections of the Bible.

Proponents of reading the apocalyptic texts in the book of Daniel, the Gospels, the Pauline Letters, and the book of Revelation as a secret code predicting the future likewise take comfort in the thought that things might be bad, but God will triumph and defeat the forces of evil. You don't have to be a prophecy buff to take comfort in this. It's a mainstream Christian belief, since the Nicene Creed tells us that Jesus will come again in glory to judge the living and the dead, and his kingdom will have no end.

But end-of-the world teachings are problematic for many reasons. The prophetic passages they inhabit are judged by biblical scholars today to be "retroactive prophecy," that is, so-called prophecies that predict things that have already taken place, not things that are in our own future. Reading seven verses in Daniel to nail down God's exit plan, or reading the book of Revelation as a work predicting the coming of an antichrist, a one-world government, and other such things presaging the end of things—all this is just so much hooey: a racket, as Barbara Rossing calls it.

This prophetic reading of Revelation has been debunked by those who understand that the book is allegorical and historical rather than predictive. M. Eugene Boring explains that Revelation is a pastoral letter written to first-century Asian Christians who were confronted by religious and political difficulty by a Christian prophet who chose to use familiar (at least to him) apocalyptic symbols and stories.[5] The great reformer Martin Luther was so concerned that people might misread the book that he considered leaving it out of his translation of the Bible, and many scholars continue to believe that to read Revelation as anything other than a pastoral letter dealing with historical events is to badly misinterpret it. Nonetheless, any discussion of the apocalyptic in the United States and in the West generally requires an acknowledgment that this method of misreading Revelation has filtered far and wide and shaped the way we view the world—even if we insist that this is not the way we view the world.

In America, shaped as it has been by evangelical Christianity, the mainstream futurist interpretation of Revelation has led us to a culture marked simultaneously by both apprehension and hope as it looks toward the future. American believers and the culture they have influenced with these beliefs assert that an actual moment is approaching when the cosmic battle between good and evil will be joined in cataclysmic fashion. This reading of the text has encouraged them to identify present or oncoming disasters that might fit their views, and to link contemporary persons to the prophecy, particularly the so-called "antichrist" (who in my lifetime has been identified as Michael Jackson, Pope John Paul II, Mikhail Gorbachev,

Saddam Hussein, and Barack Hussein Obama; some of those attributions, clearly, were off the mark).

Our popular culture also channels Revelation in this fashion in artifact after artifact; as Nicholas Guyatt observes, anyone watching movies or reading about the end of days will discover Revelation's influence.[6] Narrative elements such as the antichrist, the mark of the beast, and the general tenor of cosmic cataclysm have appeared in books, television, movies, superhero comics, and graphic novels—so where do I get off by saying they aren't true?

Well, to paraphrase a recent U.S. president, that all depends on what the meaning of "true" is. If by true we mean objective truth—that Revelation indicates that an antichrist will come to power, that all human beings will be forced to receive the mark of the beast, that a climactic battle for the ages, led by a royally pissed-off Jesus, will be fought someday on the plains of Megiddo in the Middle East—then no, these things are not "true." The passages from Daniel that led Darby to his end-times theory deal with historical events that have already happened; in Revelation 13 the beastly figure "rising out of the sea" seems to be the emperor Nero, representing the Roman Empire.

But if by "true" we mean something that tells us how things are going to be—even if it's not exactly how they're going to happen—then, yes, these apocalyptic texts are true. They tell us that someday God will fix what's gone wrong in the universe, that someday good will triumph over evil, that someday Jesus will bring those whom God loves into a world that will never end.

What does the Bible teach us about the end of the world and what follows? Most of those passages are poetic and symbolic rather than systematic, although we can glean things from the Scriptures that should give us comfort for what lies ahead. The first is that God has made us for relationship with God, and Christians believe that this relationship will not end in global cataclysm and does not end with death; Jesus died and was raised from the dead to conquer death, and this victory is universal. In his Letter to the Romans, the apostle Paul retold the story of Adam, the first human, whose sin brought death into the world, and compared his story to that of Jesus: "Therefore just as one man's trespass led to condemnation for all, so one man's act of righteousness leads to justification and life for all" (Romans 5:18).

Next, the Scriptures teach us that Jesus died and was resurrected in a physical body, and that he is the beginning of a veritable wave of resurrection that will be part of the world's remaking. Christian teaching suggests that when we ourselves are raised from the dead, we also will occupy some sort of physical body (a teaching that stands, by the way, in sharp contrast to our emphasis on eternal souls and on the separation of souls and bodies). We will not be disembodied spirits—another popular fallacy—and we will not be angels, whom the Bible describes as a sort of separate spiritual species, so get those ideas of wings and harps out of your heads. We don't exactly know what our life after death will look like—which is ironic, given the emphasis so many Christians place on getting to heaven—but I suspect it will be nothing like what we imagine, since life in the presence of God probably can't be described in words.

N. T. Wright has examined all the pertinent passages, and in an act of monumental scholarship I can only reference here, he argues that we have not understood anything Jesus was trying to teach us about the world to come. In all our talk of going away to heaven someday, we have gotten everything wrong. The Christian understanding of resurrection and life after death is truly about a new Jerusalem, Wright argues—the new heaven and new earth that God is establishing and in which we will participate. The new Jerusalem is most assuredly not some place in outer space or some other dimension, some place with streets of gold where we will live out eternity, far from earth:

> The language of heaven in the New Testament refers not to our postmortem destiny, not to our escape from this world into another one, but to God's sovereign rule coming "on earth as it is in heaven." . . . Heaven, in the Bible, is not a future destiny but the other, hidden, dimension of our ordinary life—God's dimension, if you like. God made heaven and earth; at the last, he will remake both and join them together forever.[7]

What happens if we begin to imagine a Christianity without a rapture, a religion whose entire orientation is not toward an otherworldly eternity? As shocking as these notions might be to some who have held them their whole lives, turning away from these convenient and comfortable beliefs helps us reclaim a Christianity centered on the here and now instead of on pie in the sky. It reconnects us to this earth we occupy, and to the people and things that occupy it with us, since we won't be leaving it behind to go pluck a golden harp on a fluffy cloud. It forces us to grapple with the hard kingdom teachings we discussed earlier—not to read them abstractly as a reference to heaven, but to read them concretely as something pertinent and physical, something we are called to do now.

I think my grandma, who has lived a hard life and who has not been, by any stretch of the imagination, a wealthy woman, has been looking forward to having a palace. When she dreams of a crown, it does not seem to be a metaphorical object to her; I think she can imagine the weight of it on her brow. And when she sings of walking those streets of gold someday, I think she can hear the way her footfall echoes across that precious landscape. These pervasive myths of heaven—as well as the more recent myths of rapture—have made some people content with their lot in this life, since at the end of things they can expect so much more. But as Desmond Tutu has said, teachings on such future rewards miss the point of Christianity and maybe even of earthly life itself; what people need even more than pie in the sky is pie on the ground, food for the journey, and an understanding that this life matters.

What is the gospel of Jesus Christ, and how is it the good news of the world to come? As we've already said, it isn't simply that Jesus died to save believers from hell or save them for heaven. Nor is the good news about fear, destruction, or Jesus' coming back like Ted Nugent with guns ablaze. Teachings about rapture and the judgment of an angry Jesus actually look like the things that we already know are wrong with the world: more anger, more violence, and more fear are not the remedy that God intends for us.

No, the good news is that the bad news is transient: the bad news doesn't get the last word. Suffering, hunger, war, hatred, and abusive power, which seem to have always held the field of battle, are ultimately on their way out. They are fleeting because God's master plan has been put in motion, and someday we will see how Jesus' life, death, and resurrection changed the rules forever.

In the meantime, with our imperfect faith and maybe even skepticism about the end of the world, how do we live as Christians in hope of a better future? Is there a heaven? Will we enjoy eternal life with God? Will there be a literal new heaven and new earth?

I don't know. I do hope for an afterlife that is filled with peace, love, and communion, since this life for me and for many others has been difficult. I do hope to be connected to the Creator through all eternity. But my hope cannot simply be that I will be rescued while a mass of people will roast over some archdemon's barbeque in hell.

Christianity that treats the afterlife as an escape will refuse to engage the hard facts of this life, since this world doesn't matter. And Christianity that uses the afterlife as an eternal carrot and stick is also flawed: we are called to relationship with God and with each other, not to a selfish concern about punishment or reward.

I spent my entire childhood worried that I'd be flung into the lake of fire, and my Christianity, such as it was, consisted purely of a fervent hope to escape it. Because of that, I've mostly stopped thinking about death, resurrection, heaven, and hell. Perhaps that might be a liberating act for others as well. My own understanding of the end of the world and of the life to come is simple: none of that is up to me, and the only thing I have any power over is my life here and now. How I treat others, how I engage my relationship with God, how I respect the creation that God has given us—these are the issues on which I can speak with some authority. So when someone tries to talk to me about the rapture, the final judgment, or the second coming of Christ, I tend to tell them, "I'm excited to see what will happen next."

I do believe in the second coming; I just don't know what it will look like.

And I don't try to talk my grandma out of her beliefs (in fact, I hope it's clear that I'm not here to talk anyone out of their beliefs, since trying to convince others they are wrong doesn't seem to be a thoughtful Christianity). I do resolve to walk a different path, although that leads us back to the problem that haunted us earlier. How can Christians who believe or act differently remain in communion with other Christians, even those with whom they disagree? And in a larger sense, how can we be faithful Christians in a diverse world without reaching the point where we feel obligated to kill—or be killed—for our beliefs?

In an increasingly complex world, can religion be the force for good it is supposed to be, rather than something that separates people? Can we be simultaneously true to our beliefs and still learn from those who don't share them? Our final chapter (11) suggests some possible solutions to faithfulness in a multifaith world.

For Further Discussion

1. Have you ever thought that the point of Christianity was to go to heaven and avoid hell? How much have thoughts of the afterlife shaped your own faith and practice?
2. What pervasive beliefs about the end of the world do you see presented in religious and secular culture? What things seem to be widely believed concerning the apocalypse?
3. Why would stories of approaching doom be comforting to some people? Why do so many American Christians pray for and even work for the end of the world?
4. Does the story of the rapture match your understandings of who Jesus is? Of how God works? Of how Christianity should engage with the world's suffering?
5. What hope do you claim about the end of life? What understandings of redemption and resurrection would be meaningful to you?

For Further Reflection and Study

Nicholas Guyatt, *Have a Nice Doomsday: Why Millions of Americans Are Looking Forward to the End of the World* (New York: Harper Perennial, 2007). Journalist and historian Guyatt examines the historical development of apocalyptic Christianity and takes us inside the homes and mind-sets of some of its most distinguished proponents in America.

Jonathan Kirsch, *A History of the End of the World: How the Most Controversial Book in the Bible Changed the Course of Western Civilization* (San Francisco: HarperOne, 2006). A witty and accessible study of the book of Revelation and its reception through the ages as one of the most influential texts in Western culture.

John Polkinghorne and Michael Welker, *The End of the World and the Ends of God: Science and Theology on Eschatology* (Harrisburg, PA: Trinity Press International, 2000). Some of the world's most prominent theologians and Bible scholars wrestle with the problem of the end of things, among them Polkinghorne, Kathryn Tanner, Jürgen Moltmann, and Walter Brueggemann. Challenging but rewarding reading.

Barbara R. Rossing, *The Rapture Exposed: The Message of Hope in the Book of Revelation* (Boulder, CO: Westview Press, 2004). Rossing deconstructs the pervasive Christian myths of the rapture and examines how the rapture has been at the heart of popular fiction as well as prophetic teachings. Drawing on Scripture and theology, she offers a persuasive alternative understanding of God's movement in the world and at the end of things.

N. T. Wright, *Surprised by Hope: Rethinking Heaven, the Resurrection, and the Mission of the Church* (San Francisco: HarperOne, 2008). A scholar who believes in the reality of the supernatural events described in the Bible investigates biblical teachings on resurrection and life after death. He concludes that our understanding of the afterlife has been badly off track, leading to hymns, preaching, and belief systems that perpetuate a flawed transmission of Christ's real message of the kingdom of God.

Chapter 11

Friends or Rivals?

Living in a Multifaith World

Major Ideas

1. Why some perceive faith as dangerous.
2. What problems and opportunities arise in interfaith dialogue.
3. How we can live faithfully in a multifaith world.

---

*O*n my twelve-year-old son Chandler's last visit to Austin, he spent a day seeing old friends. When I went to pick him up, I had a long conversation with his friend's father, who is, in typically Austin fashion, not a Christian. Since he has images of Hindu gods and goddesses placed around the house, I'm assuming he leans in that direction. As Chandler was putting his shoes on, the father asked me what I was writing, and so I told him I was working on this book.

"I'm trying to write a book about what it might mean to be a faithful and thoughtful follower of Christ in the twenty-first century," I told him. "Someone with a thirst for justice." He nodded, once, twice, three times. I asked about his work as a healer, and about the stock trading he has been trying as a day job. When Chandler's shoes were tied and jacket on, we parted with a handshake.

In the car, Chandler's first question was, "Were you uncomfortable?"

"Why?" I asked. I have been uncomfortable over the years around some of the more granola/patchouli/free-love denizens of Austin, but I have always liked this family, and the father, who is a gentle soul.

"Well," he said, "I just thought you might be uncomfortable because you're a really big Christian, and they don't believe like we do." I nodded thoughtfully, because I know that some Christians might be uncomfortable in close proximity to blue-skinned gods. People of any strong belief, actually, have at least a tendency to want to be around others who confirm those beliefs. But I think, slowly, I'm getting to the point where I don't require everyone to share my beliefs. In my lifetime, I have been to a couple of Jewish Passover Seders, I own a hundred-year-old Buddha statue from Thailand, and I have a translated Qur'an on my bookshelf. They are not the way to God for me, but they may be for others.

"I wasn't uncomfortable," I replied. "We had a good talk." And I smiled. "He's a good person. Who am I to tell him what he ought to believe?"

This last comment would be received as heresy by many Christians. What? You're going to allow someone to persist in error? You're going to behave with acceptance toward someone who doesn't believe as we do in the Creator of the universe? You know what's true, and you're going to damn someone to hell by not correcting him?

These ideas, whether voiced, acted on, or held in seething silence, account for many of the attacks on Christianity from those outside it. The New Atheists we discussed in the introduction (chap. 1) argue that any religion is dangerous in its truth claims because we live in a world where the worst of religion has caused terrible damage. "I honestly believe that religion is detrimental to the progress of humanity," Bill Maher said in his 2008 documentary film *Religulous*, echoing a strain of rational criticism found in many of the attacks on faith that have cropped up since 9/11. Religion that cannot tolerate any difference, insisting that everyone needs to believe as it does, is leading the world toward that Armageddon that we discussed in our last chapter. And Maher argues, because so many religious zealots anticipate the end of the world with joy, it may actually cause the end of the world. ("If there's one thing I hate more than prophecy," he says at the outset of his film, "it's self-fulfilling prophecy.")

At their heart, these critics of religion are saying that religious people seem unable to jettison their truth claims, unsubstantiated by rational evidence as they may be. But if they still want others to acknowledge the truth as they see it, religion can only be a force for ignorance, uncritical belief, and violent attempts at conversion. Sam Harris writes in *The End of Faith*, "It is no accident that religious doctrine and honest inquiry are so rarely juxtaposed in this world."[1]

This book has tried to pose an alternative both to uncritical belief and to those critical arguments against belief by suggesting that a thoughtful Christianity can amend many of the problems we discover in our faith and be, at the same time, a joyous and meaningful path to God. Certainly we are called to thought, not simply to uncritical belief, as William Sloane Coffin said: "There is nothing anti-intellectual in the leap of faith, for faith is not believing without proof, but trusting without reservation. Faith is no substitute for thinking. On the contrary, it is what makes good thinking possible."[2] The medieval theologian and thinker Anselm, whose motto was *fides quaerens intellectum* (faith seeking understanding), believed that his faith actually allowed him to get closer to the core of life's important questions.

In these pages we have wrestled with challenging concepts and applied the good minds that God has given us to reach faithful answers to difficult problems. But as hard as it might be for the champions of rationality both within the church and outside its walls to recognize, human imperfection means that our knowledge will always be imperfect. My understanding of God's revelation is the best I have now, but it is not perfect, nor is it the only understanding. So it is that Coffin, the champion of Christian intellect, recognizes its limitations and places love and compassion above it:

> It is bad religion to deify doctrines and creeds. While indispensable to religious life, doctrines and creeds are only so as signposts. Love alone is the hitching post. Doctrines, let's not forget, supported slavery and apartheid; some still support keeping women in their places and gays and lesbians in limbo. Moreover, doctrines can divide while compassion can only unite.[3]

Absolute certainty leads to thinking that if I am right, you must be wrong. Absolute certainty leads people to marginalize, hate, or attack those who believe differently. Absolute certainty leads people to fly planes into buildings, to blow themselves up on buses, and to launch wars—literal or figurative—against other faiths because they believe that God wills it. This absolute certainty is the first of the marks Charles Kimball has recognized as a sign that religion has become evil. When you and your fellow believers have the absolute, exclusive truth, other things will necessarily follow in succession: blind obedience without asking the hard questions, the end justifying the means, and ultimately "holy war."[4]

During Chandler's recent visit, we saw a mediocre animated film for children. Desperate afterward to get some value for my fifteen dollars, I asked him if the film taught us any lessons. Chandler thought for a second and shrugged, since it is not a lesson he necessarily needs: "We shouldn't be afraid of people who are different from us."

"That's a pretty good lesson," I told him. "Sometimes people end up killing each other because they haven't learned it." Robert McAfee Brown wrote that "new ideas often frighten us and make us more rigid than we need or ought to be," and certainly the contemporary world contains daunting examples of how difference can lead to difficulty.[5] So learning not to be afraid is important, and one of the ways we learn this is by being in dialogue with those we imagine as *other*. Think of your own developing understanding of the world: actually coming face-to-face with people you had only heard about (people from another race, belief system, or sexual orientation) can force you to push past prejudices and recognize a common humanity. "When we look at one another," Rowan Williams wrote, "we see not only a face that is being looked at by God, we see a person from whom God cannot bear to be parted; so how can we bear it? Any divisions in our world, class, race, church loyalty, have to be confronted with the painful truth that apparently we find it easier than God does to manage without certain bits of the human creation."[6]

One of the most positive things in the interfaith dialogue that sprang up after the 9/11 attack on the Twin Towers was that it allowed Christians and Muslims to look across the room at each other, instead of across a chasm of faith and cultural differences. It allowed them to listen to each other instead of talking at each other. And in some cases, it convinced those on both sides that one could faithfully worship God in a different way—which has always been a hard thing to acknowledge.

Although Americans have less history of people within the Christian faith killing each other, as Europe saw for centuries and Northern Ireland has seen until recently, we do have plenty of experience with Christians denigrating the faith, culture, and beliefs of other Christians. With so much conflict and misunderstanding among Christians, it should not be surprising that when we consider Christian responses to Jews, Muslims, Buddhists, Hindus, and adherents of other faiths, we often find those same emotions heightened to a greater degree. Admittedly, sometimes they are returned. Not everyone from another tradition is willing to sit down and talk, and I don't imagine that we can have meaningful dialogue with those who hate us, demean our beliefs, or do not see us as worthy of God's love.

But other people's responses to us are always going to be largely out of our control. What we can control is our approach. I want to suggest an approach that takes our own faith seriously without insisting that we hold all the answers. It looks for common ground where it exists; it does not deny our differences, but considers them through the filter of love and compassion; and it acknowledges that we are all seeking the sacred in the best way we know how.

Robert McAfee Brown has offered nine general suggestions for ecumenical exchange in this spirit of faithful but compassionate interaction. The list begins with the rejection of absolute certainty. These suggestions also include surrendering the belief that my tradition is better than your tradition, rejecting the agenda that we only dialogue so that you can ultimately see the wisdom of my position, and recognizing the cultural baggage that encompasses all our faith convictions. Further, Brown advocates the sharing of stories to recognize our common humanity, and learning of other faiths through those stories and not through outside interpreters from our own tradition. Finally, Brown says, these are matters of real urgency, since the failure to live peacefully with those unlike us, is, as the New Atheists have rightly suggested, the most immediate human threat to our race.[7]

To understand what respectful exchange might look like, we can use a meeting among people of non-Christian faiths as a laboratory that doesn't necessarily put our own issues on the line, although it certainly illuminates them. In *The Jew in the Lotus*, an account of how a delegation of Jewish rabbis from various traditions was invited to meet with the Dalai Lama, my friend Rodger Kamenetz observed some of these qualities of interfaith dialogue for which I want to argue. This meeting was, first, a dialogue between groups who were assumed to have something of value to each other; many Jews have been attracted to Buddhism as a practice, which rabbis wanted to understand, while the continuity of Jewish culture and belief during the many centuries of not having a homeland made the Dalai Lama think that their tradition had something to teach the people of Tibet. In their time together, they listened to as well as spoke to each other. What emerged from this dialogue was understanding and mutual compassion—and something spiritually powerful, as well. Rodger discovered that this dialogue and journey actually transformed him from someone only marginally Jewish into someone devoted to his faith. In other words, he did not understand who he truly was until he had engaged in this conversation with believers of a different tradition.

The group sought to understand commonalities between their faiths—the Dalai Lama had expressed an interest in Jewish contemplative practices, both cultures had experienced the difficulties of exile, and both traditions placed compassion and justice at their hearts. But this meeting did not assume agreement on all issues, illustrated by how much maneuvering it took among the rabbis of different traditions to negotiate the prayer of thanksgiving the Jewish delegation wanted to pray upon greeting the Dalai Lama, and even by the issue of how to address the Dalai Lama himself. "His Holiness" is the typical form of address, but some of the Jews (as might also be true with some Christians and Muslims) had difficulties with this honorific.

Both questions revolved around wanting to recognize this man, one of the world's great spiritual and ethical leaders, without going so far as to call him holy, since they believed only God is holy. (And while Christians might argue that we seek holiness in our spiritual journey, as we, made in the image of the holy God, seek to become ever more like God, I can see where this might be a sticking point for some Christians as well: we reverence God alone.) The Jewish delegation also rejected honorifics for the Dalai Lama that might be translated as "savior," since such a figure would seem to be involved in the act of salvation that only God can provide. One of the Jews explained the liturgical and linguistic contortions in this way: "We would like to say a word in honor—it's not that we don't want to honor—it's like saying we understand, we honor you as a source of teaching and blessing for your adherents." But not, he implied, as a savior or holy one whom Jews recognize or reverence; it was their faithful attempt to honor a great man and a great wisdom tradition while remaining true to their own beliefs.[8]

The exchanges between Jews and Buddhists on this trip were challenging, but also fruitful and necessary. Irving Greenberg, one of the Orthodox Jewish rabbis, explained why, in a pluralistic world, there is great value in interfaith dialogue: "The big question on the religious agenda is how people rooted in their own religion are able to respond to others. We must learn to affirm our truth while doing true justice to the other." Honest encounters with different modes of belief prevent a religious person from thinking he or she possesses the whole, or sole, truth. "God's will is for us to learn how to affirm our full truth [while] doing full justice to the other, not partial justice or twisted justice, or a secondhand treatment," Rabbi Greenberg said.[9]

Another rabbi, Abraham Heschel, was one of America's great heroes of interfaith dialogue; he often worked with people of other faiths on issues of common interest. He marched with Martin Luther King in the Deep South when white southern religious leaders would not be seen in his company. But as William Sloane Coffin pointed out, though it may be true that "God dwells with every committed Jew, Moslem, Christian, Buddhist, [and] Hindu who believes religious pluralism to be God's will," he was reminded that Rabbi Heschel used to say that, "the first and most important prerequisite for interfaith is faith."[10]

What Coffin meant was that I do not honor my Muslim brother or Jewish sister by pretending not to be deeply and happily Christian, nor am I taking their faith seriously if I pretend to more commonality than we possess and diminish our differences. These distinctive paths to God should be seen as distinctive; at the same time, I believe that they are worthy of honor. The Hindu sage Ramakrishna once wrote that there are many ways to climb to the roof, all of them valid; the Christian sage C. S. Lewis wrote that those of us who have already found our room in God's house should behave with great gentleness to all of those still looking for theirs. Although our first honor is to our own path, there is much we can learn from each other, not the least being that perhaps God does not call us to force others off their paths.

These last paragraphs veer precariously close to a theological belief called universalism. I am not suggesting universal salvation, exactly, although I have here quoted others who find God moving in each faithful heart. The hidden truths of salvation are, like other things, way above my pay grade; I do not know whom God will choose to redeem any more than I know what ultimate shape eternal life with God will take. All I can honestly say is that I believe I have found the path of God's love for my own life, and that I cannot imagine myself walking any other path.

But that is a long way from saying that I believe everyone else has to walk precisely where—and how—I do. The world would be greatly impoverished if that were true. I have learned from those on other paths about how to walk my own path in a more faithful and just way. I have learned from conservative Christians about claiming my faith, singing loud, worshiping passionately, and being a good steward of all I have and all I am. I have learned from Jews about holiness, setting things apart, justice, speaking truth to power, and faith in the One God. I have learned from Muslims about submission to the will of God, charity, compassion, and mystical union with the Divine. I have learned from Buddhists about inner attention, mindfulness in the present moment, gentleness, and right speaking. And I believe all of this has made me a better, more devout Christian.

When we truly see and hear others, we can paradoxically, as Brown has suggested, see ourselves more clearly. Regarding his own journey to Tibet, Rodger Kamenetz wrote that once he had seen Judaism contrasted with Tibetan Buddhism, he understood his own faith tradition as "not just an ethnicity or an identity, but a way of life, and a spiritual path, as profound as any other."[11] Encountering another faith tradition illuminated his own path and actually opened up a new life of faith for him within his own tradition. It can do the same for us.

I am writing this chapter in northern New Mexico, at the Casa del Sol retreat center at Ghost Ranch. Nearby are holy places of Catholic pilgrimage, pueblos where Native American rites and dances are still practiced on Christian holy days, a community of Sikhs, a bunch of Buddhists, a mosque, and a Muslim study center. In this landscape marked by different faiths and practices, the community that has formed around Casa del Sol has demonstrated how interfaith relations might work. A rabbi, a Muslim teacher, and a Christian minister often join to lead educational programs. They worship here, each pulling from their own traditions, learning from each other. Through their willingness to interact and dialogue, each demonstrates love and respect for other traditions. When I lead my Wisdom of the Desert retreat here each June, I speak out of my Christian tradition, relating the wisdom of Jesus, recalling the Desert mothers and fathers. But I also read Sufi Muslim stories, Jewish wisdom tales, even the occasional Buddhist saying. (Aren't those steppes deserts, after all?) I am a Christian who understands myself, my God, and my life through the window of my faith, but I often gather strength for the journey from our brothers and sisters who have found meaning elsewhere.

Our answer on how to live in a world filled with faiths and denominations is that we are not called to be, as the New Atheists would argue, less faithful, but to be *more* faithful. In response to other traditions and cultures, we are called to be more fully Christian, believing, practicing love and compassion, treating each person we meet as though that person were Christ. We are called to work with other Christians and with all those of good will to feed the poor, heal the sick, restore the damage we have done to our planet, fight for peace, and love each other. We are called to live in hope and trust. We are called to continue to believe that God is working in the world, and that this may be happening in ways that are not obvious or even recognizable.

And finally, we are called to continue journeying faithfully as followers of Christ even though others may not understand what we do or why. If we journey faithfully and thoughtfully, eventually they may understand, and eventually the negative associations that people have had with followers of Christ may drop away. Some might join us in our ecclesias; some might form new ones; others may pursue other paths. But if we live with love and compassion, all will see the connection between Jesus, the founder of our faith, and his followers—a connection that now seems to elude them. We will be doing the important work that God gives to every Christian: living so that others can see the God of Love reflected in what we say and do.

Blessings on your path; pray for me, as I will pray for you. And wherever we end up afterward, let's work for the kingdom of God now, in community, for the good of the world.

Amen.

And amen.

For Further Discussion

1. What do you feel about Christians who hold radically different beliefs? About people from other faiths?
2. How should we relate to people with whom we differ? Is it possible for people from different cultures, races, or beliefs to be friends and to honor each other's beliefs?
3. What causes religious violence? What might stop it?
4. Do you believe God redeems only Christians? Why or why not?
5. What possibilities exist in your community for interfaith dialogue? Who could your church, small group, or faith community approach about a gathering to talk about life and religion?

For Further Reflection and Study

Bruce Feiler, *Abraham: A Journey to the Heart of Three Faiths* (New York: Harper Perennial, 2004). Feiler, a Jew who has written extensively on the sometimes-violent intersection of the Abrahamic faiths in the Middle East, asks how Abraham, a figure sacred to Jews, Christians, and Muslims alike, might offer hope for dialogue and reconciliation.

Matthew Fox, *One River, Many Wells: Wisdom Springing from Global Faiths* (New York: Tarcher/Putnam, 2000). The former Catholic (now Episcopal) priest Fox mines the wisdom of faith traditions for a "deep ecumenism," finding common spiritual themes in these sacred texts and sayings from around the world.

Rodger Kamenetz, *The Jew in the Lotus: A Poet's Rediscovery of Jewish Identity in Buddhist India* (San Francisco: HarperSanFrancisco, 1994). Kamenetz records a journey by a diverse group of Jewish leaders to meet with the Dalai Lama. Along the way, they learn from each other and from the Buddhists they encounter, returning home with a new appreciation for interfaith dialogue and for their own traditions.

Rebecca Kratz Mays, ed., *Interfaith Dialogue at the Grass Roots* (Philadelphia: Ecumenical Press, 2009). This book, written from diverse perspectives, discusses actually *doing* interfaith dialogue, how it works, and the theological possibilities it presents for those involved.

Simon Wiesenthal, *The Sunflower: On the Possibilities and Limits of Forgiveness*, 2nd ed. (New York: Schocken Books, 1997). Appended to Nazi-hunter Wiesenthal's tale of how a dying SS man asked him, a Jew, for forgiveness for the atrocities he had committed, is an interfaith dialogue with responses from the Dalai Lama, Robert McAfee Brown, Abraham Joshua Heschel, and many others. The commonalities and differences in these responses to the question of forgiveness are revealing.

Notes

PREFACE

1. Scott Bader-Saye, *Following Jesus in a Culture of Fear* (Grand Rapids: Brazos Press, 2007), 28.

CHAPTER 1: INTRODUCTION: THE PROBLEM OF
CONTEMPORARY CHRISTIANITY

1. Luis Lugo et al., *U.S. Religious Landscape Survey: Religious Affiliation; Diverse and Dynamic* (Washington, DC: The Pew Forum on Religion & Public Life, 2008), http://religions.pewforum.org/pdf/report-religious-landscape-study-full .pdf. My colleagues at the Baylor Institute for Studies of Religion employ a slightly different methodology to account for our postdenominational faith, and they get a slightly different but equally disturbing figure. According to their 2005 research, published in 2006, "people 18–30 are three times more likely to have no religious affiliation (18.6%) than are persons aged 65 or older (5.4%)." Christopher Bader et al., *American Piety in the Twenty-first Century: New Insights to the Depth and Complexity of Religion in the US; Selected Findings from the Baylor Religion Survey* (Waco: Baylor Institute for Studies of Religion, September 2006), http://www .baylor.edu/content/services/document.php/33304.pdf.

2. "Survey Says: Hellbound," *The Atlantic*, February 28, 2008, http://thecurrent .theatlantic.com/archives/2008/02/survey-says-hellbound.php.

3. David Kinnaman and Gabe Lyons, *UnChristian: What a New Generation Really Thinks about Christianity . . . And Why It Matters* (Grand Rapids: Baker Books, 2007), 19.

4. Phyllis Tickle, *The Great Emergence: How Christianity Is Changing and Why* (Grand Rapids: Baker Books, 2008), 16–17.

5. Sam Harris, *The End of Faith: Religion, Terror, and the Future of Reason* (New York: W. W. Norton, 2005), 14.

6. Karen Armstrong, *The Battle for God* (New York: Ballantine Books, 2001), 33.

119

7. George Barna, *Revolution* (Carol Stream, IL: Tyndale House Pub., 2005), 30–35.

8. Marcus Borg, *The Heart of Christianity: Rediscovering a Life of Faith* (San Francisco: HarperSanFrancisco, 2003), 21.

9. Kinnaman and Lyons, *UnChristian*, 28.

10. Brian McLaren, *The Secret Message of Jesus: Uncovering the Truth That Could Change Everything* (Nashville: Thomas Nelson, 2006), 146.

11. Bob Johansen, *Get There Early: Sensing the Future to Compete in the Present* (San Francisco: Barrett-Koehler Pub., 2007), 67.

12. Garry Wills, *Head and Heart: American Christianities* (New York: Penguin Press, 2007), passim.

13. "Fundamentalism and the Modern World," *Sojourners*, March–April 2002, http://www.sojo.net/index.cfm?action=magazine.article&issue=soj0203&article=020310.

14. Diana Butler Bass, *Christianity for the Rest of Us* (New York, HarperOne, 2006), 3.

CHAPTER 2: FAITH AND BELIEF

1. David Kinnaman and Gabe Lyons, *unChristian*, 82.

2. Rowan Williams, *Tokens of Trust: An Introduction to Christian Belief* (Louisville, KY: Westminster John Knox Press, 2007), viii.

3. William Sloane Coffin, *Credo* (Louisville, KY: Westminster John Knox Press, 2004), 7.

4. Brian McLaren, *A Generous Orthodoxy* (Grand Rapids: Zondervan, 2004), 44–45.

5. Kathleen Norris, *Amazing Grace: A Vocabulary of Faith* (New York: Riverhead Books, 1998), 64–66.

CHAPTER 3: GOD: CREATOR, REDEEMER, SUSTAINER

1. Jürgen Moltmann, *History and the Triune God: Contributions to Trinitarian Theology* (New York: Crossroad, 1992), 81.

2. Ibid., 59.

3. Barbara Brown Taylor, *God in Pain: Teaching Sermons on Suffering* (Nashville: Abingdon Press, 1998), 20.

4. Thomas Aquinas, *Summa theologiae* 1.4.3.

5. Kathryn Tanner, *Jesus, Humanity and the Trinity: A Brief Systematic Theology* (Minneapolis: Fortress Press, 2001), 35–36.

6. Otto Betz, "Crucifixion," in *The Oxford Companion to the Bible*, ed. Bruce M. Metzger and Michael D. Coogan (New York: Oxford University Press, 1993), 142.

7. Rowan Williams, *Resurrection: Interpreting the Easter Gospel*, rev. ed. (Cleveland: Pilgrim Press, 2002), vii.

CHAPTER 4: THE BIBLE AND THEOLOGY

1. Williams, *Tokens of Trust*, 21.

2. Scot McKnight, *The Blue Parakeet: Rethinking How You Read the Bible* (Grand Rapids: Zondervan, 2008), 13.

3. N. T. Wright, "How Can the Bible Be Authoritative?" *Vox evangelica* 21 (1991), http://www.ntwrightpage.com/Wright_Bible_Authoritative.htm.

4. Phyllis Tickle, The Blandy Lecture, Seminary of the Southwest, Austin, Texas, September 23, 2008.

CHAPTER 5: SACRAMENTAL FAITH

1. Frank Griswold, Eckhardt Lecture, St. David's Episcopal Church, Austin, Texas, October 4, 2008.

2. Manlio Simonetti, ed., *Matthew 1–13*, Ancient Christian Commentary on Scripture (Downers Grove, IL: InterVarsity Press, 2001), 51.

3. Brian McLaren, *Finding Our Way Again: The Return of the Ancient Practices* (Nashville: Thomas Nelson, 2008), 71.

4. Williams, *Tokens of Trust*, 50.

5. Bass, *Christianity for the Rest of Us*, 213.

6. Williams, *Tokens of Trust*, 54.

CHAPTER 6: SPIRITUAL PRACTICE

1. Henlee Hulix Barnette, *A Pilgrimage of Faith: My Story* (Macon, GA: Mercer University Press, 2004), 144.

2. Griswold, Eckhardt Lecture, October 4, 2008.

3. Henry David Thoreau, *Walden and Other Writings of Henry David Thoreau*, ed. Brooks Atkinson (New York: Modern Library, 1950), 81.

CHAPTER 7: SIN AND SALVATION

1. "Are You Washed in the Blood?" words and music by Elisha A. Hoffman, 1878.

2. J. K. Rowling, *Harry Potter and the Goblet of Fire* (New York: Scholastic Press, 2000), 724.

3. Williams, *Resurrection*, xv, 16.

4. N. T. Wright, *Simply Christian: Why Christianity Makes Sense* (San Francisco: HarperSanFrancisco, 2006), 116.

5. Wright, *Simply Christian*, 10.

CHAPTER 8: ECCLESIA: THE PEOPLE OF GOD

1. Walter Brueggemann, *Mandate to Difference: An Invitation to the Contemporary Church* (Louisville, KY: Westminster John Knox Press, 2006), 1.

2. David Dark, *The Sacredness of Questioning Everything* (Grand Rapids: Zondervan, 2009), 57–59.

3. Ibid., 18.

4. Walter Brueggemann, *Mandate to Difference*, 52.

5. Desmond Tutu, *God Has a Dream: A Vision of Hope for Our Time* (New York: Doubleday/Image, 2004), 20.

CHAPTER 9: THE KINGDOM OF GOD

1. This is my retelling of Brian's story, but faithful, I think, in all the particulars; McLaren, *Secret Message*, 54–55.

2. Williams, *Tokens of Trust*, 144.

3. McLaren, *Secret Message*, 134.

4. Stanley Hauerwas, *The Peaceable Kingdom: A Primer on Christian Ethics* (South Bend, IN: University of Notre Dame Press, 1983), 62–63.

5. Amy-Jill Levine, *The Misunderstood Jew: The Church and the Scandal of the Jewish Jesus* (San Francisco: HarperSanFrancisco, 2006), 46, 51–52.

6. Bono, *On the Move: A Speech* (Nashville: Thomas Nelson, 2006), 16, 18–19.

7. Martin Luther King Jr., *Strength to Love* (1963; Philadelphia: Fortress Press, 1981), 84.

8. Jon Sobrino, *Archbishop Romero* (Maryknoll, NY: Orbis Books, 1990), 38.

9. Jim Wallis, *God's Politics: Why the Right Gets It Wrong and the Left Doesn't Get It* (New York: HarperSanFrancisco, 2005), 374.

CHAPTER 10: THE END OF THINGS

1. John Gray, *Black Mass: Apocalyptic Religion and the Death of Utopia* (London: Penguin Press, 2008), 2; Nicholas Guyatt, *Have a Nice Doomsday* (New York: Harper Perennial, 2007), 7.

2. Barbara R. Rossing, *The Rapture Exposed: The Message of Hope in the Book of Revelation* (Boulder, CO: Westview Press, 2004), 1.

3. Jonathan Kirsch, *A History of the End of the World: How the Most Controversial Book in the Bible Changed the Course of Western Civilization* (San Francisco: HarperOne, 2006), 5.

4. Raymond E. Brown, *An Introduction to the New Testament* (New York: Doubleday, 1997), 773.

5. M. Eugene Boring, *Revelation* (Louisville, KY: John Knox Press, 1989), 1.

6. Guyatt, *Have a Nice Doomsday*, 69.

7. N. T. Wright, *Surprised by Hope: Rethinking Heaven, the Resurrection, and the Mission of the Church* (San Francisco: HarperOne, 2008), 18–19.

CHAPTER 11: FRIENDS OR RIVALS? LIVING IN A MULTIFAITH WORLD

1. Harris, *End of Faith*, 105.

2. Coffin, *Credo*, 8.

3. Ibid., 9.

4. Charles Kimball, *When Religion Becomes Evil: Five Warning Signs* (San Francisco: HarperSanFrancisco, 2002), passim.

5. Robert McAfee Brown, *Speaking of Christianity: Practical Compassion, Social Justice, and Other Wonders* (Louisville, KY: Westminster John Knox Press, 1997), 120.

6. Rowan Williams, *Ponder These Things: Praying with Icons of the Virgin* (Brewster, MA: Paraclete Press, 2006), 72.

7. Brown, *Speaking of Christianity*, 117–20.

8. Rodger Kamenetz, *The Jew in the Lotus: A Poet's Rediscovery of Jewish Identity in Buddhist India* (San Francisco: HarperSanFrancisco, 1994), 46–48.

9. Ibid., 49.

10. Coffin, *Credo*, 85.

11. Ibid., 280.

About the Author

Greg Garrett is the author of a number of nonfiction books on faith and culture, including *The Gospel according to Hollywood*, *Stories from the Edge: A Theology of Grief*, and *We Get to Carry Each Other: The Gospel according to U2*; of the critically acclaimed novels *Free Bird* (named by *Publishers Weekly* and the Denver *Rocky Mountain News* as one of the best first novels of 2002), *Cycling*, and *Shame*; and of the memoirs *Crossing Myself* and *No Idea*. Greg is also the translator of Mark, Hebrews, 1 and 2 Samuel, Amos, Micah, and other books of the Bible for *The Voice* Scripture project. He has written on narrative, culture, religion, and politics for many print and Web publications including *Poets & Writers*, *Christianity Today*, *Utne Reader*, *Reform* (UK), Beliefnet, Patheos, *Relevant*, *Ethics Daily*, and *The Thoughtful Christian*, and is a featured blogger for *The Christian Century* at theotherjesus.com.

Greg is Professor of English at Baylor University in Waco, Texas, where he has received university-wide teaching honors from both the administration and the student congress. At Baylor, he teaches undergraduate and graduate classes in creative writing, American literature, film, and theology and literature. He is a licensed lay preacher in the Episcopal Church, and serves the Church as Writer in Residence to the priests and pastors in training at the Seminary of the Southwest in Austin, Texas. Greg regularly teaches, gives readings, lectures, and leads workshops and retreats across the United States and overseas. He is also a frequent media guest who has discussed religion, politics, and culture on National Public Radio, CBS Radio, BBC Radio, the Canadian Broadcasting Corporation, *Interfaith Voices,* and *The Bob Edwards Show*. He lives in Austin with his sons, Jake and Chandler.